MW00772965

Whispers From The Tomb

A True Love Story Discovered
In A Century Old Mausoleum

by Roy Widing

Whispers From The Tomb

A True Love Story Discovered In A Century Old Mausoleum

by Roy Widing

© 2019 Roy Widing

Third Edition

All rights reserved.

ISBN-13: 978-0615630564

Whispers From The Tomb

It is not the critic who counts, not the one who points out how the strong man stumbled or how the doer of deeds might have done them better. The credit belongs to the man who is actually in the arena, whose face is marred with sweat and dust and blood, who strives valiantly, who errs and comes short again and again, who knows the great enthusiasms, the great devotions, and spends himself in a worthy cause, who, if he fails, at least fails while daring greatly, so that his place shall never be with those cold and timid souls who know neither victory nor defeat.

Theodore Roosevelt

Table of Contents

Prologue

Whispers From The Tomb begins with the accidental discovery of a locked mausoleum opened once a year. Inside are two enormous marble sarcophagi standing side-by-side for more than half a century. We learn the deceased man is George Rae, a wealthy lumber baron who emigrates from Scotland as a young man. Yet little information is readily available about the mysterious woman.

Curiosity about the magnificent structure built for only two people launches a quest to know more. Whispers From The Tomb chronicles a fascinating search for details about George Rae's shadowy life, the scandalous aftermath upon his death...and the enigmatic woman lying in the tomb next to him.

Rae is historically significant because in 1890, he co-founds one of Oregon's most successful businesses, the Inman-Poulsen Lumber Company. Ample shoe leather reveals Rae's first wife, Charlotte, develops severe dementia. As a result, she's committed for years to both private and public mental asylums and dies at the state hospital for the insane in Salem, Oregon. Because her death occurs more than 75 years earlier, medical files documenting the final institutionalized years of George Rae's wife are accessible and reveal eye-opening insights. But she's not the woman lying next to George Rae...at least, anymore.

Not long after Charlotte Rae's death, George Rae marries his paramour, Elizabeth. She is younger than her new husband by nearly three decades. Their grand union on her birthday in 1914 is short-lived, for George dies less than four years later. Almost worthy of a spy novel, Rae's body is exhumed from the initial burial plot beside his first wife and spirited across the Willamette River to his final resting place

in the opulent tomb. Whispers From The Tomb next
uncovers multiple headline-making courtroom dramas. Each
involves the deceased George Rae, his massive estate and
those expecting to gain from it.

Who will receive the Rae riches? Will it be George
Rae's controversial mistress and eventual second wife? Or
his daughter, who insists she alone is the rightful heir? As
the Victorian age's conservatism lingers, problems surface
when George Rae's daughter claims Rae's second marriage
is a sham. Evidence is also provided on Rae's travels to
exotic locales with Elizabeth while still married to his first
wife. Perhaps most damning of all, Rae's daughter levels
accusations that his purported will is switched by Elizabeth,
potentially rendering it fraudulent.

Bolstering these damaging claims is testimony that
Rae marries his second wife to prevent the erstwhile mistress
from using an unevenly-enforced law of the time—the Mann
White Slave Act— against him. As a result, Elizabeth Rae
must take the stand for two grueling days. Her husband
dead, she defends her own honor and the right to his estate,
while denying sordid accusations—including the charge of
'meretricious relations.'

Whispers From The Tomb also documents the
author's journey to George Rae's Scottish hometown. There
we discover the beginnings of this fascinating story. We also
locate the final resting place of George Rae's parents and
realize their gravestones—like the interesting legacy of their
son—still stand.

Why This Book?

The United States is often considered synonymous
with opportunity. But while there is dramatic potential in
every life, few read like a bestseller. This book has many

possible titles. 'Rags to Riches.' 'True Life Romance.' 'Drama In The Courtroom.' 'Love, Lumber, Lucre & Lawsuits.' However named, it is real history. Books are written for many reasons. One involves having an historical "axe to grind." Only as a pun is that appropriate here, for this book lets the chips fall where they may.

During a riveting time in Oregon history, the central character of the story is George Rae, a man history has largely forgotten. While not a household name, Rae is a key player in one of Oregon's most successful businesses. Here you won't find an arcane analysis of wood products, the dry dissection of lumber statistics, or a pedantic primer on the timber industry. Instead, this is the story of an interesting life filled with trials, troubles and achievements. Whispers From The Tomb also chronicles a life intersecting with noteworthy events and personalities.

More modern inspirational leaders would probably have found in George Rae a kindred spirit. Like Norman Vincent Peale and Dale Carnegie, Rae is disciplined and an early day positive thinker. As a youth, Rae leaves his family and native Scotland for the United States. He later abandons job security in middle age to embark on a start-up firm— facing fierce competition—with three other like-minded men. It's his most challenging and rewarding journey of all.

Lacking much formal education, Rae appears to leap overnight from blue-collar employee to co-founder of a legendary business enterprise: The Inman-Poulsen Lumber Company. Like many "Cinderella stories," looks can be deceiving. First comes preparation and unglamorous toil.

Solid groundwork and calculated risk-taking afford Rae timely opportunity. He plans his work and works his plan. The Inman-Poulsen Lumber Company achieves astonishing success and shatters a lumber production world record in the process.

Some have suggested wealth is either inherited, the result of chance, or simply a lucky break. Here is the story of a man who makes his own breaks with preparation, hard work, follow-through and the confidence that comes with each. Rae's life embodies the adage of his contemporary, Louis Pasteur: Chance favors only the prepared mind. It's all here. The American Dream. Love. Vast wealth. Tragedy. Love rediscovered. Court battles and much more. This story deserves to be told. After nearly a century, the wait has been long enough. Here is an honest attempt to tell it plainly and truthfully.

You are like a vapour that appears for a while and then vanishes away. James 4:14

We are only passing through.   Mac MacAnally

Chapter I: Discovery

My light blue Pontiac crosses Bybee street, then coasts onto blacktop. It slows and stops between bright yellow parking stripes that radiate an eerie glow in the morning light. Another Memorial Day weekend. I step out of the car and take a deep breath. Rain-freshened air cleans my lungs like mist on the windshield. The car locked, I traverse SE 14th Street and head toward the largest mausoleum west of the Mississippi. Approaching the front gate, surroundings appear calm and familiar. Bold letters atop the entrance reassuringly proclaim: AS PERMANENT AS THE PYRAMIDS. It's a fitting hallmark to herald the time-forsaken edifice.

A fortress-like wall borders the main entry. Beyond stands a sprawling multi-story compound. Further west, windows afford distant views of downtown Portland. Just below, a sleepy marsh is infused with lifeblood tapped from that large meandering artery called the Willamette River. Inside, arched ceilings exude an appropriate cathedral effect. Earth tone paths blanket seven miles of labyrinthine walkways. These maze-like corridors lead to over 98,000 resting souls.

Along with crypts, the Portland Memorial discreetly presents a countless collection of crematory urns. They stand dutifully, secreted deep within recessed wings of a grey, honeycombed basement. Not merely different, this place is unique. Yet, even with so many distinctive traits, there is one most compelling feature. It comes from another age. The massive structure's cornerstone is laid at the close of the 19th

5

century on February 5th, 1901. This makes the Portland Memorial part mausoleum and part time capsule. While not found in many travel brochures, the Portland Memorial compares favorably to diversions now considered art or entertainment. Here is an inarguable museum of originals. The Portland Memorial is decidedly different from modern society. Absent from these grounds is the "here today, gone tomorrow" fare of culture du jour. The place has staying power and like fine wine, it has aged well.

With an elegance beyond the poshest restaurant and mystery surpassing the most baffling whodunit, the Portland Memorial will always be as fascinating as life and death themselves. The century-old monument stands weather-beaten. But sturdy cement undergirding assures rock-solid support for many decades to come. It really does appear permanent as the pyramids. Here mingles the surety of the past and unpredictability of the present. It's a strange introduction. History, meet today. Now, meet then. What was, becoming real to what is.

A Springtime Surprise

I pay respects to family members, then take an elevator several floors up and exit through a courtyard toward the mausoleum's main entrance. Looking about, I notice a stucco structure adjoining the building. It stands perhaps 20 feet square and 15 feet high, black metal gates ajar and beckoning. Within the artful wrought-iron entrance are two burnished, coppery doors. Large unlocked chains hang silently to each side. Above the entry is simply R A E. Drawn inextricably forward, I cannot turn away. Soon I'm pulling the gates back to enter.

Ancient hinges squeak softly. Eyes adjusting to the cavernous room's dimness, I meekly pass through the doorway onto an ageless marble tile floor. Vision improving, two large sarcophagi appear side-by-side before me. The names suggest they are husband and wife. The bier looks enormously heavy and not at all weathered. Indeed, everything within the building is perfectly preserved. It's as if the river of time has been completely stopped by this dam named R A E. Little imagination is needed to believe that, as completion nears, the monument's artisans may have left for one final lunch. I expect they'll return at any moment to add a finishing touch.

It somehow feels as if I'm touring abroad. Where else could such handiwork be observed? At this point in their careers, those working this stone had likely amassed half a life or more of artistic expertise. Mastery still emanates from the long-gone tools of their trade. I try to visualize them as they train and imagine a wizened instructor strolling about, hands clasped behind his back. He implores passionately, as only an artist can. "Execute from within timeless design." Forefinger stabbing at the ceiling, his voice builds. "Use only the finest materials." It reaches a quivering crescendo. "Though yours is a wordless craft, results will blare louder than the largest symphony!"

I chide myself for taking but the requisite introductory college art class. The style here carries a distinctly European motif, imbued with old world craftsmanship. It's work reminiscent of the more impressive royal tombs throughout Europe. That seems a place where the art and craft of masonry is genetic, proudly handed from one generation to the next.

A flood of thought comes autonomically, mentally transporting me to one particular tomb of Prussian royalty. It is the conspicuous yet tasteful final resting place of Imperial Germany's Queen Luise. Constructed in 1810, that impressive monument pays homage on grounds near Berlin's Charlottenburg Palace. Breathing deeply, I detect the slight scent of oranges hanging in the Spring air. Realizing I'm not in Europe but my home town, I wonder: *There's no citrus grown in Oregon.* My thoughts move haltingly. *Germany either.* Turning, I notice an aged vase emanating a fragrant aroma and question: "How long could that have been here?" Clearing historical cobwebs from my mind, I realize this tomb within the Portland Memorial was influenced by Hellenistic architecture's rebirth felt throughout 1800's Europe.

Here before me is a remnant of the neo-classical school with accents in Greek Revival style. It's as if the master himself, Friederich Schinkel, chose this place as a stage to adapt yet another creation of his favored form for the new world. I'd long been impressed by such creative muscle flexing. Schinkel was the rare one to make any design appear timeless, often with the simplest materials. Even now his work pushed the envelope of artistic possibility. The result? A surgeon's attention to detail in matters of style and substance. Such smooth finish to stone. Such lifelike portrayal. I recall a quote by Louis Nizer:

A man who works with his hands is a laborer; a man who works with his hands and his brain is a craftsman; but a man who works with his hands and his brain and his heart, is an artist.

On north and south facing walls overlooking the resting RAE's, gleeful cherubs prance in a light-hearted frieze. Several play musical instruments. The reliefs are particularly remarkable given their depth-giving appearance. It's an effect evoking a realistic three-dimensional technique. Surely a secret of the trade.

While abroad, I considered touching such works to convince myself the intricate images were real. Here, there are no security guards or cameras to hold me back. I reach

8

toward them, then catch myself out of self-conscious respect. Crown mouldings peer down, voicelessly chanting their elegance upon all who enter. I whisper to myself: If this is art representing life, what lives these must have been. Witnessing striking design with breathtaking execution, I feel as if I should have paid admission. To view it is to be overcome. Aged, yet ageless.

I also realize what the work isn't. This is no avant-garde modernist schlock and its power is enough to inspire future generations. In art galleries or mausolea, such a blissful marriage of quality design and emotion is rare. This sepulcher's union of clear vision and trance-inducing lines ensure the honeymoon will last.

The overall effect is a stunning triumph of the ideal form. In a word, flawless. In another, enchanting. A massive jolt of ironic electricity then shakes me. Here stands virtual perfection...on behalf of human existence. Above the reposed couple is a nature scene detailed in leaded-glass. A young deer stands beside a stream, ears alert. Created decades before Bambi, the resemblance is peculiar.

The chamber's logistics seem laid out with precision. With the mausoleum's southwest wing encasing the room, access is only possible from the east. Across from the tomb's entrance, the leaded-glass mural is cleverly aligned with a western window on the outer structure's stucco perimeter. Both greet the afternoon sun to maximize luminescence. "This took planning," I tell myself.

Light filters through artfully-rendered leaded glass, boldly pronouncing 'The End Of A Perfect Day' in a wooded setting. A clue perhaps? In every detail, this design betrays a creator. Expense? Not possibly an object. Now, certainly long after the director's demise, this performance is still being acted out. Those who own the stage get to produce the play. An upward glance reveals tastefully-appointed ceramic inlay. Looking down, exquisite tile-work. All around, splendor.

As afternoon approaches, ensuing arrows of solar energy find their target and penetrate any vestige of dimness. Bathed in brilliance, it's as if molten gold is ladled on everything touched by the sun. "Stunning," I whisper to myself. No other word seems appropriate. As I approach the window, ambient light scatters ethereal radiance throughout the room. Diffuse rays futilely offer their life-giving force among the reposed as I bask in the resultant glow. Come late afternoon, this aura effect could only intensify. I realize someone carefully arranged how these two were to be remembered.

As my eyes move around the room, they focus on an alcove no more than 4 feet high. Upon it rests a simple black and white photograph. Both image and gold oval frame are remarkably well-preserved. Observing the photo closely, I see a mustached, stately appearing man. His comportment indicates barely perceptible signs of an ample girth. The man's hair is parted down the middle and he wears clothes from long ago.

His demeanor appears patriarchal, inquisitive, forceful, even a little defiant. I wonder aloud: "This was someone used to getting what he wanted." My mind shifts. "Who are these people? The photo...who left it here? Does anyone visit this place?" I leave, questions unanswered. For weeks, I think about the couple and the chamber. My restless thoughts are filled with images of an earlier Oregon and now-silent people like these. Gradually they're overshadowed by work, bills and the routine of everyday life. A few months later, all is forgotten. Until the next Memorial Day.

Chapter II: Memorial Day

My parents' home is a 15 minute drive from mine. As I cross their just-hosed driveway, my father's kidding begins. "Your mother is running a little late, just like last year." A door slams and she arrives with an armful of cut flowers brimming from an assortment of old coffee cans and galvanized buckets. Dad offers a hand. "Let us help Honey; You'll hurt yourself." My Mother is unconcerned. "Oh that's alright. If you'll open the trunk, I'll set these inside and we can go. I didn't use much water, to keep things from spilling." I enter the driver's seat of their shiny Buick.

My Father shuts the trunk cover smartly, and we're off. Seat belts clicking, we leave, dust trailing down the hot gravel road. "It's supposed to be nice all weekend," I say to neither parent in particular. My Father is pleased. "Great. We'll avoid the rush. It gets so busy later." I wonder out loud: "Where do you want to start...the Portland Memorial?" My Dad ponders. "Sure. Why not there first and then over to Lincoln-Willamette? After that we can get a sandwich, then stop at the other spots."

Visiting the final resting places of loved ones is a predictable and comforting routine. It's a time set aside for reflection that allows more than a passing smile. Each stop is eased by faith. Belief in an afterlife brings the promise of seeing family and friends again. Perhaps then we'll laugh about these one-sided conversations called Memorial Day. Our schedule is always busy, but unhurried. A reflective trip to mausoleums and cemeteries, then lunch. Another round of heartfelt visits. As night falls, a peaceful repast caps the day.

I vividly remember surroundings on those first visits, weather and all. At one memorial service, I'm in shirtsleeves on a green summer day. At another, I stand half-frozen feeling winter's bite. Strange how bad weather makes death more real. No matter the season, transmogrified emotions stamp their impressions on mental cement. Those events are steps in time, touchstones in this earthly journey. The unfathomable mysteries of Heaven are enshrouded and never fully revealed. Yet they offer occasional glimpses of understanding. For now, we see through a glass, darkly. I recall my solo trip the year before, when an unexpected work appointment changed our usual routine:

"Hey Dad. Maybe they'll have that room open I told you about."

"What room is that?"

My mother looks at me. "Is that the fancy one you mentioned last year?"

"Yeah."

As we pass through the Portland Memorial's gates, it seems like I was just here. This year, across the courtyard, the Rae Room's entrance is wide open as if a lock-pick just scored big. It hits me as peculiar. My parents lag behind as I wonder aloud: "Why isn't that closed?" My Mother cocks her head to the side and responds with her own query: "Why isn't what closed?" Our strides join lockstep, then slow in tandem to a stop at the building's entry. Brightness streams through the chamber like sunlight piercing clouds. Crossing more than one threshold, our feet nervously shuffle, echoing as we enter. We stand and marvel at our surroundings. Moments later, a very different sound fills the cavernous tomb.

"Can I help you?" It's a businesslike voice, low but friendly. I nearly jump, then stammer: "Oh. We're visiting for Memorial Day. The doors were open." "Certainly," nods the distinguished sixty-ish man. He continues in a clipped accent. "Welcome to the Rae Room. There's quite a tale here. I presume you're not familiar with it." "No," my Mother offers. "Very well. Details have been gleaned and passed down over the years. It's now an oral tradition, of sorts." He proceeds to introduce himself with a name soon forgotten. Given his overall demeanor, I later dub him Mr. English. He continues after a pensive pause.

"This gentleman, Mr. George Rae, was quite a businessman. A timber baron, to be precise. Word is that he ran off with the maid, whose name was Elizabeth. That's her next to him. His family is said to have had some hard feelings about their acquaintance. It was quite a scandal at the time." "I can imagine," agrees my father, himself born the same year Mr. Rae passed on. 1918. The final year of the Great War, the war to end all wars. It's eerily coincidental. The end of this man's life marks the start of my own relatable beginnings. "The age difference alone says a lot," volunteers my mother.

English continues. "There are 26 years between the couple." Hand sweeping across the room, English proudly states: "The cost to build this structure was estimated a while back. It approaches seven figures in today's currency." A long whistle flutters from my Father's mouth. "There is much agreement among conservators, that for its time, this memorial is among the most splendid in the state, if not the entire Northwest. Provision has been made to allow public visitation of the chamber each year."

As English speaks, he breathes life into two people deceased for many decades. Like how the couple's marriage raises eyebrows, she being his maid and so much younger. About another wife, buried across the river. And his fabulous wealth. As we leave and thank our host, I step outside and am struck by the incongruity of bright sunlight. This is how bats must feel.

Yet in a strange way it's as if I've been watching
The Wizard of Oz in reverse, for some especially vivid parts
of this story seem to center around the tomb. In my den a
few weeks later, I replay events from the Rae Room.
Leaning back in a swivel chair, I wonder: "Why would
someone spend so much...and go to so much bother? Simply
to be remembered? There's got to be more to it than that."

Pencil tapping the desk in steady cadence, I consider
the likelihood of learning anything more. I'd never been too
interested in mysteries. Maybe because those I've read seem
contrived. Or perhaps I'm just too impatient to sit through all
the twists and turns of what is often an improbable outcome.
Truth seems so much more interesting.

"Call it what you want," I tell myself. "This Rae
thing is not fiction." Before long, I'm hooked and with good
reason. For starters—and unlike most mysteries—here is not
one dead body, but two. Then there's the magnificent tomb
they inhabit. That by itself is enough of a head-scratcher to
make anyone curious. Add a much younger woman. And
finally there's the wealth. Judging by the tomb alone, there
was plenty. I decide to research the situation and put in
motion a hard to imagine journey. My sojourn first takes me
to Portland's Multnomah County library, the grand dame of
local information. It is huge and very old.

Because libraries contain an overwhelming amount of
data, right away I determine to sift in an organized manner. I
narrow my search to sections likely to provide ready answers.
Newspaper accounts seem a good place to start. Silently, I
wonder: *Maybe I'll get lucky here and learn more about
George Rae...something to explain such a monument.* I have
a name, some dates and little else.

Once inside the library, I attack a flight of pale
marble stairs leading to the newspaper archives. If Rae was

well-known in these parts, this place should confirm it. Filing cabinets reveal tray upon tray of neatly categorized information a century or more old. Inside are rows of black plastic microfilm containers, each resembling a charred cigarette pack on steroids. "Bizarre," I murmur while rubbing a hand over my stubbled face. It's Saturday morning, a nice time to avoid shaving.

My search begins. Oregon Daily Journal: 1900-1901. Oregon Daily Journal: 1902-1903. On it goes. Finally, I corner my quarry—Oregon Daily Journal: 1918-1919. "Bingo," I whisper. Slipping a microfilm roll into a nearby machine initiates the tedious but sometime fascinating task of scrolling through recorded history. Witnessing events so long ago is akin to stepping into a time machine. Advertisements, the *lingua franca* of any newspaper, are rife. They include the strange—like corsets for sale, soap mugs and mustache wax—but also the familiar, like food, tobacco and other still-common goods, like bicycles. But these bikes don't look quite like the trusty old Schwinn I had as a boy and certainly not at all like today's models.

Clutching dates scribbled down in the Rae Room, I look up continuously in a furtive attempt to match those on the screen before me. "There," I say to myself, pointing at the date: February 12, 1918. "That's on Rae's tomb. Here's where the digging begins." Even as the storm of World War I quiets, much European news coverage continues. Passing over the newspaper index for now, I scan the Oregon Daily Journal, page by page. Attempting to grasp a feel for the time, I tell myself: "Pretend to be a reader of the day—as if I'm alive then." Given the vantage of foreknowledge, it is virtually impossible.

To George G. Rae, events during his life on earth stand frozen in time, with nothing experienced past February, 1918. His is now a suspended world. I consider that for

those like George Rae, not only is World War I forever
current...World War II never existed. Nor Prohibition, the
Great Depression, or even the historic solo flight of Charles
Lindbergh, much less John Glenn. Completely forget
television, the Korean conflict, advances in civil rights, the
Vietnam war, both Kennedy assassinations. Moon walks.
The Berlin Wall's rise and fall. And how would one explain
the Internet to someone in 1918? I'm astounded at the
changes.

And while we both might call Portland "home,"
George Rae and I are indeed from different worlds. Sitting at
the library table, I realize if he were sitting here with me,
words common as penicillin or Stalin would be meaningless.
But the things *he* experienced. The Pacific Northwest's
natural beauty fills my mind. In 1918, Oregonians witness
teeming salmon runs and unfettered views of a territory now
dotted with asphalt streets and concrete towers.

"So much wealth," I observe. "He must have had
quite a life." Scrolling through a few more microfilmed
newspapers, I locate his obituary in The Oregon Daily
Journal's February 14th edition. I'm pleased to recall
February 14th, 1859 as the coincidental date of Oregon's
statehood. Before long, pieces of the puzzle begin to fit, as
the newspaper article confirms English's 'timber baron'
remark. The obituary looks fairly typical and includes a
photo like the one in the tomb.

George G. Rae, who died at his home, 189 1/2
Sixteenth street North, last Tuesday night, was born in Ellon,
Scotland, and came to New York when a young man. From
there he went to San Francisco, but did not remain long.
Forty-five years ago he came to Portland, where he had
since resided. For 14 years he was yard manager for the
Willamette Steam Mills. With R. D. Inman and J. Poulsen, he

founded the Inman-Poulsen Mill in the Spring of 1890. Though retiring from active business 12 years ago, he still retained his interest in the mill.

Further down it reads: "...member of the Republican party and Episcopal church." At first I tell myself: "Nothing unusual here, I suppose." But then I read: "...Shriner and Mason..." I tell myself: "Hmmm...Those records would be interesting." Given the secretive reputation of certain fraternal groups, I temporarily surrender hopes of locating any dusty old manuscripts to shed light on George Rae. Those organizations eventually respond to my queries about this mysterious man. Given my dwindling list of clues, when they do reply with little information from so long ago, my response is visceral: "Snake eyes. Dang!" It becomes an oft-repeated refrain.

Since decades have passed, I'm disappointed, yet not really surprised, by the dearth of records. I recall the mural of wooded tranquility in his burial chamber and realize here was a guy who loved what he did. I find little else that day, but leave feeling satisfied. Months later in a small public library near my home, I uncover one possible explanation for the Rae tomb's design. It's in a book called Scotland: Cultures of The World:

...wealthy Victorians...built huge monuments to their dead. One surviving example of this is the necropolis in Glasgow, which contains 3,500 tombs and many more graves of modest sizes. The tombs have been a major tourist attraction for over 100 years.

I consider several pieces of this illuminating information. *The Necropolis in Glasgow. Wealthy Victorians. Huge monuments to their dead.* Especially intriguing is that as a mid-1800's Scotsman, Rae is a subject of Queen Victoria and he certainly died wealthy. But with

English's estimate of the tomb's cost, this possible explanation for such extravagance still seems far-fetched. My thoughts race. "The detail... the planning. For what? Love? It's just too pat. And this goes way beyond ego. But why?" My thirst for insight is not so easily slaked.

Trudging up several flights of library stairs on a hunch, it feels as if I'm climbing a mountain. In a way, I am. Only this is a mountain of information. My reason for returning is the mountaineer's mantra. Because it is there. On the third floor, I discover a trove of books on the region. Perched patiently on their shelves for just such an occasion, they are chronicles of local history. While modern directories are computerized, what I'm after can only be found through more manual means. The bright room stings me with excitement as I make a beeline for the card files and whisper "R...R...R...where are the R's...."

Heavy oak cardholders play traffic cop on this lonesome road through Oregon history. These files prove to be a vital research tool, since they cross-reference people and events in newspapers and books of the day. Included are articles on every topic imaginable. Water rate hikes. Election coverage. Lawmakers and lawbreakers. Marriage announcements. Obituaries. Almost everything. But what makes them especially valuable to me is their local slant on events so long ago.

I tell myself: "These records are my passport to this region's past." I pull one file's curved brass handle and begin rummaging. Each old handwritten entry adds suspense. Soon, I'm imbued with a tangible sense of mortality, for in my hands is stark evidence of time's passing. I wonder silently: *This faded writing surely survives its author. Can it remain legible much longer?*

I work slowly through the cards. One says 'Rae, George' on it. I jot alphanumeric codes on a scrap of paper, then walk to a stack of books. I need both hands to grasp the thick volume's spine. It slides unceremoniously off the shelf. Called 'History of Oregon,' the hefty yellowed tome features local personalities back to the state's earliest days. An index at the back of the book reveals an entry with Rae's name. I begin to read. Several paragraphs and a now-familiar photo bring alive the once-sketchy outline of a man from long ago.

George G. Rae, who was long prominently identified with the lumber industry in the northwest and for many years made his home in Portland, there passed away on the 12th of February, 1918, in his seventy-fifth year....He became one of the organizers of the Inman-Poulsen Lumber Company, of which he was made vice president.

This company has the record of cutting more lumber in a two-year period than any other one-side mill in the world. He never regretted his determination to seek a home and fortune in the United States, for he here found the business opportunities which led him steadily upward until he gained a most substantial position among the leading business men and lumber dealers of the northwest.

It ends, confirming his wealth:

His efforts featured in the utilization of the natural resources of this section of the country and in the up-building of the state, and the proof of his individual business powers and capability was seen in the prosperity which ultimately crowned his efforts.

While not the mother lode, it is a nice gold nugget. I'm buoyed by new clues to an old mystery and leave the library hoping that more luck and work will provide answers about the life and mystery surrounding George Rae.

Chapter III: The Journey

In 1843, Scotland is a jewel in the British Crown and
Queen Victoria reigns. On a July day in the northern Scottish
town of Ellon, John and Isabelle Rae become parents to a son
they name George. The lad is christened barely a month
later. His early years are spent with two brothers and three
sisters. It's an orderly existence between the bookends of
siblings and school.

By 1861, George Rae is a single 18 year old resident
of Ellon's pastoral river region known as Meadow of
Waterton. His father co-owns and manages Mitchell & Rae
Grain & Manure Works in nearby Aberdeenshire, Ellon.
George works there as a merchant's apprentice. At this place
and time, vocations are passed down from father to son. The
youth is thus born into a dilemma. This son of a Scottish
manure merchant could assume the family trade, or cut his
own path. Will the young man follow his father's vocation?
Rae the younger is about to parlay his pedestrian prospects
into astounding success of a different sort.

In 19th century Scotland, those working close to the
soil commonly remain near their native village. Young
George can be called many things, but common he is not. As
a subject of Her Majesty during the glory days, the seafarer's
tales beckon. Indeed, it is largely with assistance from
colonies like Scotland that Brittania rules the waves and a
great deal more. A generation before, this ocean-going
power spawns a new America.

Given such global dominion, the United Kingdom
draws upon prodigious sources of manpower and materiel.
The Union Jack flies over substantial portions of India,
Africa and Asia. So vast are her territories, the sun doesn't
set on the British Empire. She is the envy of the age. During
this exciting era, George Rae is interested in more than

geopolitics. A hunger for new experiences gnaws at the soul of young men like him. Rae cares deeply for his family, yet he desperately yearns for adventure. Abroad is excitement and opportunity in a world he's heard about but never seen.

Tested by restlessness, his familial bonds yield. In 1869 at the age of 26, George Rae answers his life-changing dilemma in bold fashion and steps aboard a wooden ship leaving bonny Scotland. Sails set for the United States, his journey has begun. Now loosed from pier and past, Rae's mind is free to race with the craft as it departs for open ocean. Behind is all he has known. Ahead, uncertainty.

But George Rae is a friend of adventure. The ship sails through different kinds of weather, a telling metaphor for his life ahead. Waves lapping the craft, he pauses as if to consider this unfolding dream becoming reality. When Rae disembarks the vessel, change is in the air and he arrives to a bustling United States.

The Civil War's guns have been silent but four years and the country is rebuilding. He soon finds employment and before long meets a woman barely 20 years old. Her name is Charlotte, but she's often called Lottie. In 1875, George Rae becomes a naturalized U.S. citizen. That same year, he takes Lottie as his wife. George is now father to Lottie's 10 year old daughter, Edna.

Around this time, newspaperman Horace Greeley writes persuasively about golden opportunities out west. It's a risky trip to this wild frontier. Indian battles rage and many never complete the brutal journey. But survivors enjoy many rewards. George Rae sees a way to improve his young family's situation.

Around 1877, the Rae's arrive in California, and by 1882 settle in Portland, Oregon. Unlike the New York and

San Francisco they leave behind, much of Oregon is rural
and untamed. Portland is also home to a growing population.
Fueling this growth are numerous sawmills. Trees felled in
Portland along the Willamette River's banks explain its other
name: Stumptown. It's the setting for an exciting life ahead.

Declining Returns

After months of work, my research on George Rae
begins to deliver less and less. Given such effort, I still know
surprisingly little about the mysterious man in a fantastic
tomb. Discouraged, I question how much material could still
exist about a private person now gone for nearly a century.
Viewing microfilm one morning at Portland's main library,
I'm particularly depressed. With no leads in sight, I've hit an
especially dead end. Spurring myself on, I plead:
"Something. Then I'll quit."

Barely noticing the newspaper article, I pass over it.
Hand reversing the machine's smooth worn grey metal lever,
the microfilm changes directions, then stops. My as-yet un-
caffeinated mind sluggishly processes the page. In front of
me is the first real clue of how history has treated George G.
Rae. Oddly enough, it's located in a newspaper story filed
almost 2 years after his passing. Dated January 20, 1920, the
article has surprisingly little to say about his life—or even
death. Instead it has to do with the probate of his estate.
Having searched so long for a payoff, I don't yet fathom the
treasure before me in a headline shouting across the decades:

Rae Is Forced To Wed housekeeper declares Amme.

**Fear Of Prosecution Under Mann White Slave Act Led
To Marriage, witness tells court.**

Too excited to stop reading and make a photocopy, I
scribble the article down verbatim, in case I lose my place:

Further statements to the effect that the late George Rae had told him prior to his marriage to his former housekeeper that he was forced to take that step because he feared she would make trouble for him under the Mann White Slave Act was offered before Judge Tazwell this morning by Edmond G. Amme, Attorney & relative by marriage to Rae's first wife.

I finish reading and realize the story is not only gaining speed, it's now shifting gears. I recall English's remark about a scandal and whisper "Talk about an understatement." Because George Rae's life lacks the key ingredient of surviving witnesses, I ponder the chance of finding relatives who know the story behind all this. It's a fleeting, improbable thought. Yet, my enthusiasm is renewed by this fresh paper trail in a new direction. The sleuth in me is invigorated.

As my next target, I place a bead on legal documents to locate family members mentioned in the article. Marriage, divorce and death certificates could help corroborate events and fill many gaps. Perhaps then I can also grasp more about Rae's life from the extensive detail usually contained in wills, deeds and articles of incorporation...if they even exist and I'm lucky enough to find them.

A Courthouse Journey

Weeks later during a stroll down SW Columbia Street in the hot Portland sun, I pause, take a deep breath and sigh. "Here goes." Climbing a flight of steps, I enter the Multnomah County courthouse and am greeted by buzzing sounds and a row of metal detectors. The situation's surreal nature grips me. Here I am, about to step back in time to investigate happenings of long ago. Yet, to do it, I must pass through machinery of the modern age. I walk cow-like through the squeeze-chute of a security contraption. The question "What would Mr. Rae think about this?" sears my mind like a branding iron.

After a round of errant elevator rides and stairway hikes, I find myself back on the first floor. During my gauntlet, I learn files on estates clear back to the 1800's are in the records department near the entrance. On my way there, I pass a trio of pistol packing Multnomah County Sheriff Deputies and am thankful to be armed only with directions. As they cautiously eye my notepad, I wonder if I resemble an attorney they don't like and turn a hallway corner. There between me and the records I seek stands a vintage *film noir* door, replete with oak frame and opaque glass. "Looks official enough," I opine.

Inside, the line is long. Beneath a low ceiling and sallow lighting, I wait amid a sea of law clerks and legal assistants. Yet not all there are button-down types. A few scruffy-looking youths in front of the line seem familiar, even bored with the routine. I look at my watch and wonder if anyone in the queue could possibly be working on a project as old as mine. Time passes with equal parts boredom and inadvertent eavesdropping. Most in line request information on pending court hearings. Then it's my turn.

I step forward and hand the lanky clerk a completed requisition slip. I hear "1918?" and nod "Yes." Spinning around, he confidently strides back a few steps and his hand goes skyward beside a tall file cabinet. Studying the microfilm container's label, he looks up, sounding like someone who'd just found a lost sock. "Here it is!" I reason he's either lucky, or knows his department. The clerk walks me to an adjoining room. There, he details the temperament of one particular microfilm viewer before leaving. I thread the roll as shown. Things get interesting in a hurry.

IN THE MATTER OF THE ESTATE OF GEORGE RAYE, DECEASED

reads the microfilmed document, followed by a subheading "Petition and Complaint in contest." First confused by George Rae's misspelled last name in the document's heading, I realize the paperwork is thick for a reason. This is the challenge of a lumber baron's estate. And within the document at every opportunity, the validity of George Rae's will is assailed.

...that said purported will, dated December 9th, 1914, above mentioned, is not and never was the last will and testament of said George Rae, deceased. That at the time of the execution of said writing...George Rae was acting under the coercion, duress, undue influence, misrepresentations and fraud of said Elizabeth E. Rae, and that...Elizabeth E. Rae procured...George Rae to execute said will in her favor and to disinherit your petitioner by force, coercion, duress, misrepresentations, and fraud practiced upon the said George Rae, and by false and fraudulent statements and beliefs created in the mind of said George Rae against your petitioner, [Maud Rae Emerson];

As accusations fly, I'm entranced with a realization such scurrilous claims surround the two people long at rest inside the Rae Room. I wasn't expecting this and continue reading.

...that for a number of years prior to the execution of said will and prior to the pretended marriage of said George Rae and the said Elizabeth E. Rae, the relations between said George Rae and Elizabeth E. Rae had been meretricious, and...Elizabeth E. Rae had through said relation secured from...George Rae large sums of money and had forced [him] to convey to her property of large value and had by coercion and threats placed...George Rae in fear of her and

*had induced him by such means to disregard his obligation
and duty towards your petitioner [Maud Emerson] and had
poisoned the mind of said George Rae against...[Maud
Emerson]...and had induced him and attempted to compel
him to transfer a large amount of his property to [Elizabeth
E. Rae] and to execute the will in question so that the said
Elizabeth E. Rae should inherit and acquire the property of
the said George Rae to the exclusion of your petitioner.*

The summary speaks volumes:

*That prior to the execution of said will, [George
Rae] had made a will in which practically the entire
estate...had been left to your petitioner, and that if it had not
been for the undue influence and coercion of the said
Elizabeth E. Rae, your petitioner would have inherited
practically all of the estate...*

The Big Picture

Details from my research helps to make sense of
Mr. Rae's circumstances. Seven years after George Rae first
marries, his oldest teenaged step-daughter Edna marries a
man named Job Hatfield. Eight years later, Job Hatfield and
George Rae comprise the lesser-known half of a company
they co-found with two other men, Robert Inman and Johan
Poulsen. Their firm becomes known as the Inman-Poulsen
Lumber Company, a source of fantastic wealth for the
owners.

Within the Rae family, one particular person appears
at odds with the rest. She is a daughter George and Lottie
Rae adopt later in their lives and her name is Maud Rae. The
girl is two decades younger than the Rae's oldest daughter
Edna. From what I can tell, Maud Rae is portrayed as a real
live wire. In 1912, Maud marries a man named Theodore
Seth Emerson.

Early in 1914 things get complicated when George Rae's first wife Lottie passes away. Late that same year, George Rae marries his second wife, Elizabeth, his former maid. Several years later, George Rae dies. In the will that surfaces, his adopted daughter Maud gets virtually nothing from George Rae's estate, so she fights for the inheritance. Who will win the battle for the Rae riches? As the situation unfolds, I'm spellbound. Maybe I do like mysteries after all. I survey the events before me and mentally walk through the situation.

George's adopted daughter Maud Rae Emerson plans on getting it all. But when her mother dies and her dad falls in love with Elizabeth, Maud is out of luck. No wonder she's upset enough to sue her father's estate. She gets ten lousy bucks when she might have inherited close to a hundred grand. I consider how much that must have bought back in 1918 and realize Elizabeth must have been a charming woman to garner so much of George's loyalty.

I then ponder the relationship between George Rae and his daughter Maud—the one who originally expected to inherit the Rae riches. Convincing evidence will be necessary to execute the Emerson legal team's 'switched will' theory. If they can't prove the existence of a purported second will, the Emerson's expose a glaring chink in their legal armor. Yet this is precisely what they announce:

...that the exact provisions and contents of such prior will your petitioner is not able to state, but alleges that the said Elizabeth E. Rae had access to the safety deposit box of the said deceased, George Rae, and abstracted therefrom numerous papers either immediately prior or subsequent to the death of said George Rae, but your petitioner is informed and believes that the contents thereof can be established in case the same has been destroyed.

Paging through the document, I'm a bit shocked by Maud and T.S. Emerson's boldness to accuse Elizabeth of replacing the original will with a phony document. I read further. Finally comes the astounding request:

...the said pretended will dated December 9, 1914, is void and should be cancelled and annulled by this Honorable Court for the reasons above set forth.

Related documents reveal beneficiaries of George Rae's estate are compelled to testify before the court to argue why each should receive a portion of the inheritance. Sorting through George Rae's essential disinheritance of his daughter Maud, what first appears as a shift in his loyalties turns perplexing. It seems a departure from what I had perceived as the man's own unwritten code. Perhaps I was wrong about him.

I eventually realize that once George Rae's youngest daughter Maud marries in 1912, his sense of obligation realigns. As a consequence, Rae perhaps feels his daughter no longer needs his money, or is no longer entitled to his estate. As I learn more about these people, each develops a patina of individuality that shines through dimming decades of death, dollars and presumably, devotion.

Driving to work a few days later, I replay this true-life drama. Reviewing such events more than a half-century old leaves me with a wide range of considerations. In the big picture, George's actions appear understandable. What wealthy widower wouldn't appreciate a youthful companion in his waning years?

Elizabeth is a sunny summer day against the prospect of a lone, cold winter. Court documents also note George Rae's health isn't great. As a result, he appears to drown his sorrow with the elixir of love. Rae's daughter, Maud, behaves somewhat predictably as well, out of financial self-interest. Or is that *all* that's driving her?

Given later sordid accusations hurled against George Rae, I'm amused with each discovery of George Rae's kind acts. Ever-fond for the land of his youth, George Rae returns to Europe late in life. With compassion for needy family members there, Rae wills his elderly sisters a nice stipend upon his death. His devotion reaches out to each of them, loyal from beyond the grave. Humble beginnings and a lifetime of separation don't diminish Rae's sense of duty to kith and kin. But it's Elizabeth that captures his heart and potentially his treasure.

I find myself wondering whether money is the sole motivator in Maud Rae Emerson's challenge to George Rae's estate. Even with the story's unfolding scandals, at this point I feel obligated to initially give Rae's second wife Elizabeth the benefit of any doubt, then answer raised concerns as I go. *So she was the housekeeper.* Fine, I figure. That's honest work. *So she was younger than the man she married.* It happens all the time. *So they wed.* George Rae was probably lonely, if not grief-stricken.

Their relationship might not raise an eyebrow today, but peering through eyes of the time is a different matter. What am I to make of certain details, like George and Elizabeth's joint travel arrangements prior to their marriage, when George is still married to Charlotte? Yet for all I know, Elizabeth may have lived the life of a saint. And what of her life after George's demise? She survives him by nearly 25 years. Yet there she is, right next to him. Seems loyal to me, I conclude.

A Young Maud Rae
Photo courtesy of Oregon Historical Society

Lifted carelessly, my file-laden briefcase on this story now has sufficient heft to necessitate a chiropractic adjustment. I don't move it much, unless necessary. It eventually triples in size and later converted to a much larger portable file cabinet. Flipping back the rectangular box's clear plastic top one evening, my fingers trace over a dozen files, each growing in size.

For months now, I've gone it alone and find no surviving relatives. No witnesses. No one with an inside view. Yet I still long for the big break: A surviving—even if distant—relative with ties to this intriguing story. But with such a cold trail, I now concentrate on less personal links to George Rae and consider connections to his co-founders.

One possible lead I consider is H. B. (Henry Brooks) Van Duzer, erstwhile president of the Inman-Poulsen Lumber Company. Van Duzer is now best-remembered for the treed corridor that sports his name between Portland and Lincoln City on the Oregon coast. In life, he gains respect for his leadership of both Inman-Poulsen and the Oregon Highway Department.

Like Inman-Poulsen co-founder Job Hatfield, Van Duzer is also buried at Portland's Riverview Cemetery. Coincidentally, Riverview may also hold clues to what could be the initial burial site of George Rae. I decide to pay a visit. Classic wet Portland weather accompanies me.

Inside the Riverview office, an attentive staff member summons a detailed map and confirms the burial of several key members of the Rae story. I then note mention of a 'Charles Rae.' The only problem is that 'Charles Rae' has no headstone. Yet according to the cemetery map, he rested right next to George Rae's first wife, Charlotte. With no headstone extant, could this be the spot from where George Rae was exhumed as Mr. English suggested?

With my luck on a roll, I decide to double down. I ask for and receive directions to H. B. Van Duzer's gravesite. It's a short stroll from the Rae family's graves. The marker of this former Inman-Poulsen chief executive says

frustratingly little and the surprisingly modest headstone
yields but his name and time on earth. "Snake eyes again," I
tell myself. "Dang!" Walking through rustling leaves on my
way to the car, I'm approached by a young woman and hear
"Can I help you?" By clothing and countenance, I suspect
she's a salesperson.

A nagging question about a different Inman-Poulsen
executive comes to mind and before realizing it, I hear
myself respond. "Why yes, as a matter of fact." That's
because months earlier, I'd visited Job Hatfield's grave
monument just down the hill. On the back side of his
obelisk-shaped head stone is a name and it isn't his. The
inscription reveals a child interred just years earlier.

We walk to the grave marker. I point to the
unfamiliar name and ask: "What is such a recent inscription
doing on the headstone of a man buried in 1900?" She
chooses her words carefully. "There are very strict
guidelines for situations like this. My guess is that it must be
a close relative. I can check our files for family members
and let you know what I find."

With persistence, several weeks later I have a name
and address. It's not easy, but after a bit more work, I track
down a telephone number. In this instance, I'm doubly
fortunate, because Lynda Lockwood is related to not one, but
two Inman-Poulsen co-founders. Lynda is a great-
granddaughter of Job Hatfield. This also makes her a great-
great-granddaughter of George Rae. I call Lynda. She is
pleasant, helpful and interested. We arrange to meet on a
Saturday morning. Though I arrive a little late at their tidy
two-story on a cul-de-sac in the suburbs of greater Portland,
Lynda and her husband DeLoi are most gracious.

After introductions, I learn Lynda's family is familiar
with fame. Her mother, Jenie Jackson, found stardom in

television (The Wild, Wild West) & film (Ride The High Country) during the 1960's and 1970's. I explain to Lynda and her husband of my quest for information about George Rae and the Inman-Poulsen Lumber Company. Before long, I realize we each hold different pieces to a fascinating puzzle.

Lynda confirms the child named on Hatfield's monument is a descendent of Inman-Poulsen co-founder Job Hatfield. Lynda also tells me that her own family research confirms George Rae was indeed buried in February of 1918 in Riverview Cemetery, only to be later exhumed, moved across the river and re-entombed within the majestic final resting place of the Portland Memorial's Rae Room.

"That explains the phantom grave," I mention and recall my confusion at seeing the name 'Charles Rae' on the cemetery map. It now made perfect sense. George Rae's headstone was missing since the misnamed Rae was indeed moved—clear across the river to the Portland Memorial. A closer examination of George Rae's obituary also confirms his initial burial in Riverview Cemetery, just like Mr. English explained during my early visit inside the Rae tomb.

Before I leave, Lynda provides a most promising lead. It's the phone number of another surviving relative, a Mrs. Edna Phelps. She too has a direct connection to the Rae story. Mrs. Phelps' maiden name is Amme. As daughter of attorney Edwin Amme, Edna's father represents George Rae's daughter Maud and her husband T.S. Emerson against George Rae's second wife Elizabeth in the fight for the Rae estate.

As I dial Edna's phone number, I'm not sure what to expect. The line rings and I wonder how she will respond to a stranger's keen interest in her ancestry. Given my pleasant experience with Lynda and Deloi, I convince myself it's alright, then hear the click of a phone being answered. The

voice on the other end confirms I am indeed speaking with
Edna Phelps. I explain my attempts to better understand her
relatives from the past and perhaps grasp events in the Rae
battle. As a child at that time, she remembers little. Before
we hang up, I inquire about someone she is certain to
remember—her father, Emerson attorney Edwin Amme.

"What do you remember about those times….did
your father ever mention any details?"

"I recall him saying George Rae built a home for his
mistress…"

Remembering a reference to Elizabeth's property in
court files, I jot myself a note to check tax records, as they
typically confirm construction dates. The date I find is 1906.
That's around eight years before George and Elizabeth wed
and when George's commitment to her may have become as
solid as the home's foundation. Follow-up meetings reveal
Mrs. Phelps to be both a pleasant and helpful link to the Rae
story. She opens for me a trunk filled with photos and
newspaper clippings about her family, each one more
interesting than the last. And while she's a senior citizen, her
memory appears solid.

The Search Continues

Over time, I develop a sense about each cast
member in this long-forgotten play. Most of their
motivations I seem to understand. Others, try as I may, I
cannot. I also begin to wonder if it's simple curiosity that
attracts and holds me to this story of two long-deceased
souls? This couple yearning to be together, never to be
separated?

The story that began with my discovery of two
entombed people still seems like simple curiosity to me, with

beguiling elements of classic literature. Yet whenever I feel like quitting, it's not curiosity alone that keeps me going. What *does* spur me on is this story's love angle. Especially powerful is the sheer humanity of two people so wanting to remain together that a magnificent shrine is constructed as a monument to their love. The Rae Room may not be the Taj Mahal, but in some ways the sentiment is the same.

Perhaps it's the romantic in me. What begins as a lark is now a serious challenge. By this point I've also abandoned any concern that my search for answers might appear like a bizarre predilection for the long-deceased. Each clue, however subtle, also gives weight to Elizabeth Rae's frustratingly light footprints. Finding fresh details about her is now a Herculean task. Yet I hold out hope to detect any existing remnants before the ravages of time remove what few traces remain.

Analyzing the options, I realize my best chance to glean what survives of this elusive woman lies waiting for me back in the Multnomah County library's newspaper archives. This is because due to her exceedingly low profile, the only existing record likely to provide details would be her obituary. Before long, I'm hovering over a drawer full of microfilm boxes. I scan their labels: Oregon Daily Journal September 1-15, 1942...Oregon Daily Journal September 16-30, 1942... Oregon Daily Journal October 1-15, 1942... Oregon Daily Journal October 16-31, 1942...

"That's it!" I grab the microfiche packet, practically running to the closest available machine. Opening the box, I thread the round plastic microfilm roll onto the machine's bright blue take-up spool. My eyes remain fixed on the screen above. With microfilm machines humming in the background, I announce in a low tone: "October, 1942. Let's see: Elizabeth passes away October 24th..."

As I search, a distant era is chronicled before me. "Rommel Driven Back" proclaims one headline. "Rationing To Continue" says another. Minutes later, I sort through it all to find a notice published the day after her death. Not even an obituary, it's so small I almost miss it. Save for the impressive tomb and her name on some legal papers, it seems as if Elizabeth Rae never existed.

RAE-Oct. 24, Elizabeth E. Rae, 1522 SE 21st.
Friends invited to attend services Tuesday, 2:30 P. M., at
Chapel of the Portland Mausoleum, SE 14th and Bybee.
Edward Holman & Son, The House of Holman, Hawthorne
blvd. at 27th, Directors.

It's not a lot, but at this point I'll take anything I find. With so few options, I rack my brain for other possible sources of information about this mysterious woman in the Rae saga. The state Bureau of Vital Statistics was a big help while researching my own genealogy. The only problem now is the required proof of kinship to receive a death certificate. Since I'm not a relative, the chances seem bleak. Dejected, I moan: "Stumped again."

Mulling the situation over in my mind, I then recall records more than 75 years old are considered archives of historical significance. As public documents, anyone can access them. My attitude adjusted, I rejoice: "Just the break I need!"

Anxious walks to the post office become a daily ritual. On a damp Saturday evening in late June, I arrive at my post office box. Opening the tiny square gold-colored door reveals the death certificate of Elizabeth Rae. The official-looking form provides considerable insight into her life. Specifically, it confirms that Elizabeth remains single for nearly a quarter century before her own death.

Given her relative youth, she no doubt has many opportunities to remarry. I tell myself: "This squelches the likelihood of her marrying only for money. If she did it once, she'd have no problem doing it again. I guess there's no 'black widow' here." If nothing else, Elizabeth's position as George's true-blue companion seems assured.

Thanks to this recent discovery, before long I'm to learn more about this woman who captures George Rae's heart in a different century. As a result, the drama's quiescence is solidly jostled from slumber. Long-dormant personalities now leap off the page, revived. Some very strong characters will reveal their roles in this play. My fascination deepens with each act. For every question answered, several more are raised.

With company namesakes Robert Inman & Johan Poulsen at center-stage during certain scenes, the limelight of providence is not always focused on George Rae. But even as he stands in the shadow of their fame, so bright is the reflective glare of success as to bestow him abundance. Attentive views from the front row will offer a glimpse into the little-known life of a private man.

Chapter IV: The Portland Memorial

In time, I learn celebrity is one of many surprises
within the Portland Memorial's hallowed halls. Fame is
indeed part of Oregon history. That's because not far from
the Rae Room, Mayo Methot shares a niche with her parents.
Mayo who? At another time, she's known as the 'Portland
Rosebud.' Mayo Methot becomes a celebrated actress, but is
now more famous as Mrs. Humphrey Bogart, well before
husband Bogie meets future wife Lauren Bacall. Then
Mayo's world forever changes.

This unusual connection between Hollywood and
Portland has me cracking open a few books on the man, his
career and wife Mayo. The cinematic legacy of actor
Humphrey Bogart is one of an emotionally distant toughie
with a soft side. Mayo and Humphrey are known as the
'Battling Bogarts,' a moniker arising from their legendary
fights. Mayo is busy as a professional in the theatre during
the 1920's and her major movie work occurs during the
1930's. Humphrey Bogart also works the theatre, then
becomes huge in film from the early 1940's into the 1950's.
One star rising, another falling.

Mayo is said to deliver a great right hook. Bogie
even calls his beloved boat 'Sluggy' in her honor. Numerous
arguments, thrown bottles and all, reportedly occur aboard
Mayo's namesake. Today it's difficult to pause at Mayo's
crypt without reflecting on both the zenith —and nadir—of
her career. Though she achieves stardom in theatre and film,
her life story is now obscured by time's veil and the shadow
of a more famous husband.

Mayo Methot was born in 1904. Some documents
name Portland, Oregon as her birthplace. Her death
certificate, with information given by her mother, says she
was born in Chicago, Illinois. Her family settles in Portland,

Oregon where young Mayo gains years of child stage experience in Portland area theatre productions.

In 1919, Mayo graduates from Portland's prestigious private Catlin School, later renamed Catlin Gabel. She leaves Oregon for a small part in a Lionel Barrymore film with William Randolph Hearst's Cosmopolitan Pictures. In 1921, Mayo marries Cosmopolitan Pictures cameraman John Lamond in Vancouver, Washington. They divorce in 1927.

From 1927 to 1930, Mayo is busy in theatre with strong parts. Along with 'Torch Song,' she's in the hit 'Great Day,' singing the lines of that show's big number: "More than you know, more than you know, Man of my heart, I love you so…" In 1931, Mayo marries Percy T. Morgan, the son of a wealthy banker. They divorce in 1937.

At the 1936 annual Screen Actors Guild dinner in downtown L.A.'s Biltmore Hotel, Mayo reportedly meets an up-and-coming movie talent named Humphrey Bogart. Those unfamiliar with Bogart need only know that he eventually becomes one of Hollywood's all-time biggest stars. Their cinematic careers meld as Bogart & Methot work together in the 1937 film 'Marked Woman' starring Bette Davis. Later, after an early spate of gangster films, Bogart becomes the man to whom war-time audiences can relate. His best-known performances carry the thumbprint of a loner trying to make good. Bogart is cast as the iconic 'stand up' guy, who when the chips are down, does the right thing.

Given his extraordinary stage presence and talent, Bogart finds fame in a wide variety of films. Some of the more famous ones are 'To Have And Have Not,' (co-starring Lauren 'Betty' Bacall, who in real life eventually replaces Mayo as Bogart's wife), 'The Maltese Falcon,' 'Casablanca,' 'The African Queen' and 'The Caine Mutiny.' Portland's

Mayo Methot indeed makes the big time, performing before audiences in New York and the cameras of Hollywood. She even marries an international star. But by the time Bogie leaves Mayo for Lauren Bacall, her troubled life worsens. Half a decade later, Mayo dies in 1951 at the age of 47.

Mayo Methot circa 1930
© The Ben Solowey Collection. All Rights Reserved.

Her family now gone, too, it seems sad. The one who gave life to lines composed by others now has nobody to speak for her. The theme is familiar. Virtual unknown becomes the object of worldwide attention. Top of the world, but not for long. For Mayo Methot, the staying power of celebrity wanes like applause at the end of a performance. The Mayo of show biz is now the punch line to a Hollywood trivia question and a footnote on the pages of fame.

For years after her death, a dozen roses arrive at her crypt each week. It's rumored Bogart sends them. In 1957 when Bogart passes away, Mayo's flowers reportedly stop arriving at the Portland Memorial. Oregon borders California geographically, but the glitz and glamour of Hollywood seems far from Portland, Oregon. I ponder why Mayo's life story isn't 'local girl makes good,' since that's not how she's remembered to most. Reality is harsh, the reason clear. It's mainly because she doesn't keep the guy.

Mausoleum Moments

Celebrities are interesting. Yet my own curiosity tends more toward the forgotten and unknown, for drama lingers in untold stories. Like the appeal of Tutankhamun's tomb, unexplored territory provides exciting possibilities. Like artifacts lying preserved on the ocean floor, the unsolved is waiting to be discovered. For every examined Titanic, there are countless unexamined shipwrecks. And while often hard to fathom, every one holds the promise of dazzling treasure.

Whether shipwreck, boy king or lumber baron, each offers a unique insight of humanity. If the unexamined life is not worth living, examining the unfamiliar life offers more than a standard rehash of the same names and faces. The Rae Room is a monument to a multi-faceted tale of love, intrigue, wealth and a natural for the armchair sleuth. My journey on the trail of George Rae's life continues and is to offer much about a colorful past.

Death is not always recognized as what it is. Natural,

inevitable, universal. Walking through the mausoleum's halls, more than once my Dad remarks: "I'm pretty sure I used to caddy for him during the '30's." Or "This man was a well-known attorney." Or doctor. Or businessman. Here, literally shoulder to shoulder, are those from every station of life.

History. Local, relatable and always here to consider. In a macabre sense, like library books stacked perennially on a shelf. But unlike a library, these shelves always remain full. Nor is there a mausoleum Dewey decimal system, with say, engineers here and nurses over there. Aside from obvious family connections, it's more akin to a long day trap shooting, where the spent shells of lives lie strewn about in no particular order, in seeming disarray.

A walk through the Portland Memorial is an escape from one fast-moving world to another of quietude for both the quick and the dead. On virtually every stone of slate, granite or marble are entries etched into the diary of generations. Fads don't reveal themselves, yet trends clearly do. No hoop skirts or bouffants to observe. Lots of Elk, Mason and Shriner symbols, though.

Groups once burgeoning with growth now languish. Yet, with their emblems on so many crypts, the loyalty of their diehard members is hard to miss. A journey through the compound's maze of walkways conjures history. Some inscriptions are clean of much more than a name and lifespan. Others count multiple memberships, organizations and causes. Prominent on many crypts are accomplishments held high.

Veteran's tombs divulge name, rank and branch of service. Around certain holidays, there are also flags—lots of flags. Sometimes mentioned is a faraway place where the supreme sacrifice was made. Grieving families are understandably proud. Here rests a representative panoply of humanity, from virtually every nationality, creed, race and belief. The sheer magnitude of the place is humbling. For it's one thing to observe memorials of contemporaries, side by side, having shared life's common times and events. But it's quite another to behold entire generations faded from this globe, lives never intersecting to touch the era of each other.

Yet reality bespeaks that among those departed, the distance between 1, 10, or even 100 years isn't so much as a decimal point shuffle. It takes a place this peerless to comprehend the finite nature of earthly existence. From visitor to resident in one heartbeat. Like cremations held on the premises, here the bonds of time are consumed and shrivel like the driest tinder in a roaring bonfire.

While hard to grasp by mere mortals, centuries of separation must seem insignificant to a supreme being unrestricted by the dimension of time. The Portland Memorial represents both the adventures of yesteryear and the adventurers themselves. Like the vast frontier that awaits astronauts on a launch pad, it is an immense, unimaginable trek. Vehicle and destination differ, yet both involve unfamiliar terrain. My promenade continues.

Passing into a main hallway, I hesitate before more resting multitudes, each frozen in an age-old, yet timeless ice-age. All around me are columns of crypts. My breath escaping, I whisper awestruck: "The collective experiences of all these people." The sea of time's never ending waves crash unremittingly upon this most mysterious of human coastlines. Words above a passageway testify in silent agreement:

This is the trysting place of the seen and unseen
The frontier between here and there
It is earth's most sacred place Dr. Edward H. Pence

I've been here often. My wish is always the same. *But to know their stories.* To comprehend hard-earned chapters penned by minds and hearts now silent. Turning these pages in time is like discovering an unread book, as each experience is again new. Placing my hand on the front of a granite tomb before me, I sense both text and texture. Lives reviewed, whether in story, old letter or newspaper clipping, are alive once more, vicariously as if new.

This stately building is achievement's final repository. Here lie the performers of amazing feats, where the grandest accomplishments oft go untold. These trailblazers through time carry to their graves cumulative centuries of wisdom, libraries of life-benefiting knowledge. Though silent, they speak powerfully of humanity, now in another form. As we are, they once were. As they are, we too shall be.

Book nor life can be judged by the cover. Yet while inadequate, epitaphs are humanity's shorthand. Like the pearl inside an oyster, meaningful lives are treasures easily passed over. Here, each stone etching hints of the unseen. There is so much to have learned from others now gone. They leave behind instructive experiences and forgotten blessings. But even their sad lessons from life's storms possess power to teach, right wrongs and encourage those certain theirs is the heaviest burden.

I stop to consider the human condition, so vast with virtually infinite possibilities, directions and outcomes. Those here had beginnings and middles, too. Important to remember when surrounded by perpetual displays commemorating life's end. Highs and lows. They include the crypt of a man with plenty of degrees. And the child of poor parents never experiencing that exciting first day on campus. Stops and starts. The epitaph revealing an education in courage, not from books or lectures, but through fear in a foxhole. A few steps away, flowers blossom for a loved one, dead half a century.

Crossing that teetering bridge to an unhuman void, the strongest and wisest soul is rendered pathetically impotent. With each epitaph encountered, the chasm broadens. All so undeniably out of reach. For the prepared, it means traveling light and walking in it, too. I resolve faith is the only passport worth carrying for the journey every person faces alone.

More Mysteries

With some lines of inquiry exhausted, I ponder other clues to pursue. Then it hits me. What lead could be more basic than the headstones of George Rae's associates? I wonder if some of them might rest near where I started, at the Portland Memorial's Rae Room. Late on a foggy winter morning, I hike the steps up to the Portland Memorial's front office.

A receptionist behind a large desk greets me. I explain my trip through local history and am introduced to a neatly attired woman in business suit and high heels. She casually glances at the short list of names I hand to her. "Would you like me to help you find these?" "That would be great," I respond. Heading to an adjacent room, she comments over her shoulder: "I just got back from lunch...let me get my coat." I clutch the list of names and dates, unsure what these precious clue shards might summon. My palms sweat in anticipation of discoveries I realize can only found here.

We leave the warm office and cross a paved walk through a mist of light rain. First on my list is Inman-Poulsen Lumber Company president George Thatcher. Thatcher was a son-in-law of company co-founder Johan

Poulsen and worked for the firm over 25 years, serving as president from 1929-1934. But there is another reason for my interest in Thatcher. It stems from his being named executor for the sizable estates of Inman-Poulsen co-founders like R. D. Inman, Johan Poulsen and George Rae. Their selection of future Inman-Poulsen president George Thatcher as executor of their estates is a good example of the strong bonds between the firm's executives.

These three Inman-Poulsen 'heavy-hitters' are in a position to choose virtually anyone for the important task of handling their substantial estates. To a man, they select George Thatcher. Among esteemed pillars of trust, Thatcher is perhaps the most trusted of all, for he's the guardian of wealth others spend a lifetime attaining. It seems Thatcher is duly rewarded for his efforts, for when George Rae's co-founder R. D. Inman dies in 1920, Inman's will states:

...I give, devise and bequeath to George W. Thatcher, of Portland, Oregon, and his heirs, my certain new Winton roadster automobile, model 1920.

Considering Inman's wealth, astonishing mechanical ability and former position as president of the Oregon Motoring Association, there's little doubt the new car George Thatcher receives is a fine one. I'm also curious to see how George Thatcher's resting place will juxtapose with other executives from his firm.

My guide leads me to a very old carpeted room called a columbarium. Looking around the room, we step back in time to surroundings nearly a century old. Showcased inside are hundreds of cremation canisters, each displayed within a clear glass case. It takes a few minutes, but we find George Thatcher's niche. Once we do, I stand humbled before a very old, golden crematory urn. It includes the name of his wife, Kate, the daughter of Inman-Poulsen co-founder Johan

Poulsen. While larger than some of the other containers, it's an unexpectedly modest monument to such a respected man. "Amazing," is all I can muster. We move along.

Descending stairs, we next enter a cold, stark basement and proceed to a wing I never knew existed. This section would be difficult to locate without assistance. Strolling the grey corridors, our breath hangs in the winter air. On the walk to each crypt, we chat as I try to better understand details about the Portland Memorial. As we approach the last few, my guide voices curiosity. "What's the name of the company you're researching?" "The Inman-Poulsen Lumber Company," I say. "They started in Portland around 1890." Looking up, she responds with emphasis. "There are lots of lumber people here. *Lots.*"

Now deep within the old wing, my guide first locates Johan Poulsen, then Robert Inman. Before leaving she asks: "Is there anything else I can help you with?" Wanting time alone to observe possible clues, I respond with "No, thanks. I'll just take some notes and then find my way out. Thank you again for all your help." She hands me her business card. "Sure. If you have any questions, feel free to stop back at the front desk."

As my guide leaves, I sense few signs of recent visitors. I realize it's Winter, but deep in this old wing, even artificial flowers are sparse. The spartan niche of Johan Poulsen and his wife Dora face the main walk. Around a corner, his business partner Robert Inman and family now reside within a gated area before a stained glass mural. Even in death, these two company co-founders remain close.

While Inman and Poulsen have elegant resting places, they reside in what might kindly be called tight quarters within a distant section of the Portland Memorial. This contrasts with the opulence and prime location of the Rae

Room, an entire main-level addition situated near high traffic entry doors and dedicated to but two people.

A century earlier, west-facing windows near Inman and Poulsen's crypts would have offered a sweeping panorama of the Willamette River and downtown Portland. To those visiting the final resting place of these two lumber pioneers, the view is now obscured by...trees. I take a few photos and then some notes. The visit gives me a lot to think about. I leave knowing a little bit more about these partners of George Rae.

Chapter V: Early Lumber Days

Each small clue I uncover makes George Rae more three-dimensional. In time, it becomes easier for me to visualize his day-to-day life and the backdrop of events around him. On more than one evening, I drift off to sleep, my final conscious moments awash in everyday sensations of 19th century Oregon. Dust from dream-induced hoof-beats fills my lungs and I feel the need to cough. Stagecoach drivers holler and clatter me along on jolting paths.

While asleep, I sense six-shooters gushing grey-white curls of smoke and gunpowder's unmistakable odor. But for early Portlanders, it is not a dream. Those pedestrians stride along creaking boardwalks as storefronts greet them with disparate aromas. Pungent tobaccos assault noses with the subtlety of a Bowie knife. A few doors down, the husky leather scent of boots, holsters and saddles hangs in the air. Further down the street, fresh-sawed lumber exudes its minty fragrance. Once awake, I wonder how Oregonians of yesteryear would perceive their beloved state today.

Were these pioneers to revisit the land they settled, they'd likely be amazed at the changes during their slumber. Arriving in the present, this wouldn't be their first time adjusting to unfamiliar surroundings. If their past is any indication, these hearty souls would wipe sleep from their eyes and soon find productive work. They'd once again forge new ideas, improve on old ways and blaze fresh trails. Like Lewis & Clark before them, pioneers by their very nature seek to view from undiscovered vistas.

More than a century ago, Oregon's lumber leaders walked now-familiar streets. Today, names like Yeon and Weidler grace Portland's signs and bestow hard-earned honor. As we commemorate their lives on avenues, monuments and maps, these touchstones double as compasses, directing from the past. The accomplishments of earlier Oregonians instill a sense of direction. Often overlooked but never really gone, these early citizens still lead the way. To a handful of the ponderous, obscure names like Inman, Poulsen, Rae and Hatfield kindle a curiosity to understand lives of people long ago. To many, these mysterious monikers are rarely considered. To all, their deeds become more unfathomable with each passing year.

The majority of Oregon lumber workers are never famous, just hard-working. As testimony to such effort, their labor builds thriving businesses, magnificent buildings and countless charities, while at the same time battling epochal adversities of danger, disease and death. Whether shopkeeper, mill-worker or company president, necessity stokes their imaginations, smoldering with creativity.

These potent constructive forces team with optimism's heady adrenaline, tethered by the disciplines of hardship, hard work and plain pioneer faith. It's a daunting inheritance and our benefactors' legacy is a tough act to follow. Conceding the difficulty, some among us accept their unspoken challenge to go one better.

While the accomplishments of our forebears are impressive, like us, their torches are sparked by those walking before them. We all have help from earlier trailblazers. In the process, past and present are illuminated. Their lives—and ours—align with the words of Sir Isaac Newton: *If I see further than most, it is because I stand on the shoulders of giants.*

A Sense Of The Time

My focus on Oregon's lumber past begins simply enough in an encounter with the Rae room. Eventually, I'm flooded with reams of documents. There may be a limited amount of material written about George Rae, but I discover there's plenty on his industry. My search on Rae and the company he co-founds is akin to finding a splinter in the forest. There are records of countless lumber firms through many decades and sifting through that unordered mass in hopes of locating additional information on the man is sheer toil.

So much lumber-related material is available, I narrow my focus to get a handle on such massive volumes of information. I eventually limit my research to the years between 1890 and 1918, for these are particularly noteworthy years of George Rae's life in Portland. Each hard-fought success—whether a discovered photo, or an insightful article that points me in a fresh direction—keeps me going. In the process, I recognize familiar planets in a vast universe. The constellation includes Oregon history, lumber history and the Inman-Poulsen Lumber Company. Like stars on Orion's belt, sometimes the three are difficult to differentiate. Researching George Rae is an education in each.

Lumber Lore

Dissecting lumber history reveals much, so I dig deeper into lumber's Northwest past. This industry I'd often taken for granted leaves a huge impact on the region. There's a never-ending association between life and lumber here. From the very beginning, Native Americans use trees for canoes, bows, arrows, fire, and shelter. Many years later, timber remains central to the economy and culture.

Peeling the bark of time from the lumber industry's inner cambium exposes two elements common to most businesses, transportation and labor. They are industry's xylem and phloem, the lumber trade's equivalent of botanical lifeblood. Throughout Oregon's past, timber-laden vessels transport logs with a history rich as the cargo in their holds. And what could be more American than labor unions? In reviewing the lumber industry, plenty of fascinating topics stand out and it's hard not to repeatedly walk down what might simply be a pleasant diversion.

I eventually realize that to know what makes George Rae tick, I need to educate myself about both his times and occupation. One interesting feature I discover is about life in the woods, or "timber culture." Like any lifestyle, it is multi-faceted, claims a unique slang and own set of values.

Among rugged woodsmen, camp life reflects a sense of order and ritual. Details differ by location, but in logging camp dining halls, breakfast tables groan with oatmeal, ham, bacon, eggs and cooked potatoes. Flapjacks are piled high and served with steaming mugs of coffee to start the day. A good cook is king. So unless meals are appreciated by the men, a new chef is quickly found.

One other element of camp life includes workers with the colorful title of "whistle punks." Their job is to safely signal the movement of timber. Each of these informational tidbits serves up a colorful slice of life from a lumber industry long ago.

Shifting Gears

In 1806, changes begin around the Northwest after Lewis & Clark cross the North American continent. A growing population by the mid-1800's sees an expansion of the west coast lumber trade, even before the advent of a reliable railroad line. With no easy way to send lumber cross-country, there are many mills and much competition. Unless transported by waterway, timber is processed locally in mills close to where it will be used.

Machinery is a good barometer of logging's progress and efficiency. For much of the 19th century, horsepower literally means power from sure-footed steeds or oxen. Then around 1881, naval engineer John Dolbeer invents a logging engine patterned after an auxiliary motor found on ships of the time called a "donkey." It eventually replaces animal power. Fueled by wood, these steam engines are a superbly efficient way to move logs through forests. Donkey engines are rigged with a winch and easily skid logs over rugged terrain.

Because of relatively easy waterway access to the Pacific Ocean, for years foreign lumber sales are actually more important to the Pacific Northwest economy than trade with neighboring American states. Lumber becomes the engine that runs Northwest commerce. Throughout this period, the lumber business is genuinely competitive. Many factors work against a monopolistic trend. They include a spread-out resource for mills to draw upon, low barriers to entry and new federal "trust-busting" laws. Historian Thomas R. Cox comments on these early days in his book Mills And Markets-A History of the [P]acific Coast Lumber Industry to 1900:

...no John D. Rockefeller, no Standard Oil emerged to bring order into the chaos that was the uncertain, highly competitive world of the cargo mills. Then, and in the years to come, the lumber industry remained fragmented, perhaps the most purely competitive of any major industry in the United States.

Large lumber firms throughout the U.S. recognize the Northwest's potential later than in other industries. Timber is not yet concentrated in the hands of a few. Companies like Weyerhauser and Georgia-Pacific will become important players, but that is many years away. Until the days of efficient nationwide transportation and manpower, local companies dominate. This is their time and opportunity is everywhere. By the time George Rae arrives in 1870's Portland, lumberman George Weidler's mill on Savier Street cuts 50,000 feet of lumber a day. Laid end to end, this amount of lumber stretches over nine miles. The district is located near the Willamette River in an area known as 'Slabtown,' so-called for large cuts of wood piled throughout the area.

Weidler's operation eventually becomes the Willamette Steam Mills Lumbering and Manufacturing Company. As I slog through information related to George Rae and the Inman-Poulsen Company, there's a surprising amount of documentation on Willamette Steam Mills and for good reason. It keeps popping up throughout my research as one of the region's earliest and better run sawmills.

Three noteworthy men become acquainted while employed at the Willamette Steam Mills during this time: Robert Inman, Johan Poulsen and George Rae. A penchant for excellence is cultivated by the men's association with Weidler. Willamette Steam Mills grows into a large company world-renowned for quality. Co-owned by George Weidler and railroad magnate Ben Holladay, this groundbreaking firm sets the standard for later Oregon sawmills. Historian Thomas Cox confirms this in a quote from a February, 1880 communique:

The lumber carried to Hong Kong on the Coloma and Alden Besse was well received. It had been produced at George W. Weidler's Willamette Steam Mills Lumbering and Manufacturing Company, a firm noted for up-to-date equipment and quality products. Allen Noyes reported, "Mr. Spratt who purchased my lumber said...[it] cannot be beaten."

Experience in generating such fine results at a large operation has the effect of 'raising the bar' for the future Inman-Poulsen co-founders. Weidler's philosophy of producing a high caliber product has a lasting effect on his employees. However, work at Willamette Steam Mills is not always rosy. Many years later, Johan Poulsen comments on his tenure there:

I wrote letters to a number of large mills throughout the United States and was offered a position which I accepted by the Willamette Steel Mills Lumbering & Manufacturing Company, of which Ben Holladay and George Weidler were owners...At that time the mill was worth quite a good deal less than nothing, as it was heavily mortgaged. However, prosperous times came and it began making money, which resulted in litigation between Ben Holladay and his brother Joe. A receiver was appointed and I finally got tired of having lawyers and others constantly going through the books and interrupting my work. I had been there nine years. I quit and went to work for the North Pacific Lumber company. I worked for it three and a half years and then decided to go into business for myself.

Upon leaving Willamette Steam Mills, the future Inman-Poulsen Lumber Co. executives take with them big mill experience. Given this know-how, Inman-Poulsen's co-founders find expanding production and facilities a natural progression from the very start. This keeps their new firm growing at a time when increasing capacity is an especially wise move in an era of heightened lumber consumption. The Portland Oregonian's January 1, 1882 edition states the Inman-Poulsen mill is able to produce *...every style of lumber available anywhere.* Finished products like doors, sash and mouldings yield the company a greater profit than rough-hewn lumber and enhance the firm's bottom line.

Chapter VI: Inman-Poulsen

1890 brings a formal partnership between Robert Inman, Johan Poulsen, George Rae and Job Hatfield. Inman becomes President and Johan Poulsen is named both secretary and treasurer of the Inman-Poulsen Lumber Company. Why Rae and Hatfield's names aren't headline material remains unclear. One version has it that, realizing the unwieldy nature of such a lengthy moniker, the men impose a two-name limit and draw straws. Another has a coin toss determining the firm's enduring name.

The Inman-Poulsen Lumber Company constructs their first mill on the east bank of Portland's Willamette River, not far from its confluence with the mighty Columbia. With access to the Pacific Ocean, this location grants the firm a strategic staging point for efficient timber transport. Beginning with a capacity of 35,000 feet of sawed lumber per day, output eventually increases twenty-fold with 700 workers employed. But Inman-Poulsen's owners have a serious problem early on, later acknowledged by Johan Poulsen:

Back in 1890, R. D. Inman, George Rae, J. Hatfield and I leased the ground here and began buying logs to saw into lumber to supply the local market. Before we had been in business a month some of the other mill men decided to put us out of business...we had mortgaged our homes to raise the money to get this plant so when it came to being put out of business there was a decided difference of opinion on the subject.

But muscle from competitors isn't the only problem they face in the early years. On Thanksgiving Day, November 1896, fire destroys the Inman-Poulsen sawmill. Instead of going out of business, owners Inman, Poulsen, Rae

& Hatfield have new facilities up and running in two months. The new mill is even bigger than the one it replaces, with an annual capacity of 200,000,000 feet.

In mustering a competitive spirit against misfortune, this 'can-do' credo imbues Inman-Poulsen with even more success. Aided by their hands-on mill experience, the co-founders are gifted with insights to oversee their employees. They know what to do and how to do it. But while the company is empowered by experience, clues suggest a surprising ace up the co-founder's sleeves. With four divergent personalities and backgrounds around the corporate helm, Inman-Poulsen has a symmetrical synergy of management depth and breadth.

Instead of a liability, this cross-pollination of corporate styles is a distinct benefit to the Inman-Poulsen Lumber Company. Unlike countless businesses that burn out from executive friction, Inman-Poulsen's executives work together in a complementary manner. A unique personal chemistry supports their corporate approach, especially rare in the rough and tumble business of late 19th century lumbering. Collaboration and cooperation are central to this 'cutting edge' corporate model. Most elemental is that each man specializes in a central aspect of the lumber operation. At Inman-Poulsen, the co-founders provide unique strengths.

Who Were These Guys?

Robert Inman's forte is machinery. Early on, he designs, operates and repairs the physical plant at Inman-Poulsen Lumber Company, holding patents to numerous inventions. Johan Poulsen's attention to detail in all things financial gives Inman-Poulsen another distinct edge. Known for a watchful eye to the bottom line, his talents include balancing books and cutting costs. Blessed with Inman's engineering prowess and Poulsen's managerial know-how, a crucial component is still needed to nail down Inman-Poulsen's lead among the region's mills. That area is sales— a key factor for business success. Underscoring the value of this position, co-founder Johan Poulsen later recalls the daunting challenge their fledgling company faces at this critical juncture: "We were forced to enlarge our market to keep in business." In the early years, Inman-Poulsen's options are simple. Either sell more lumber, or close down. Sales must grow or they lose it all. Backs solidly against the wall, the partners rise to the occasion.

To represent the company, extraordinary talents are needed. The head of sales for their emerging firm will need ambassadorial skills to help develop the business growth they seek. Trust and charisma are key. The position requires an affable personality under certain instances, a hard-nose when necessary and judgment to know the difference. Simply put, the company needs someone who is both a 'people person' and industry expert.

Enter George Rae

By 1890, George Rae has a background in various positions with different lumber firms, including millhand, timekeeper and sales-yard foreman. His experience with different companies and clients brings the steady hand of confidence to a position vital for Inman-Poulsen's future. Rae provides the spark vital to every successful business. It is professional salesmanship and he supplies it in spades. Rae's potential appears early in his lumber career. Carey's encyclopedic "History of Oregon" plainly underscores Rae's persuasive powers and business acumen: "Not long after...[being hired]...he was given charge of the yards as salesman." But even George Rae can not do it all single-handedly. As evidence of their teamwork, co-founder Johan Poulsen also develops associations with lumber customers in the western United States and Asia:

...I wrote letters to friends of mine throughout the Northwest, and we soon began selling lumber in Utah and elsewhere. About once a year we would ship a little dab of lumber aboard the Coloma to Shanghai. We also made an occasional shipment to California coast points.

Inman-Poulsen's co-founders collectively lash their futures to one another, providing the stability of a log raft. From the beginning, each man's trust in himself and his co-founders is among their most plentiful commodities. Johan Poulsen later describes the attitude enabling their success:

Overcoming obstacles develops character. We had faith in the future. As a matter of fact, we had to have faith and courage or we never could have made it, for we went up against some pretty strenuous opposition.

Character. Faith. Courage. It helps that Inman-Poulsen Lumber Company's founders are independent, strong-willed men. A side benefit of the firm's collaborative management style is continuity of succession. For half a century at the Inman-Poulsen Lumber Company, near-seamless executive transitions are the norm. Consistent leadership becomes one of the company's distinguishing traits.

Throughout much of its reign, the firm essentially operates as a quasi-family business. From the beginning, maturity and corporate chemistry among management affords trustworthy input and mutual support in high-level decisions. The four co-founders look after one another, getting along like protective big brothers. Examples abound.

Inman-Poulsen co-founder Job Hatfield marries George Rae's daughter, Edna. George Rae arranges son-in-law Job Hatfield's burial, even assisting in the purchase of the grave. Future Inman-Poulsen president George Thatcher marries Johan Poulsen's daughter, Kate. But it doesn't stop there.

George Thatcher, Johan Poulsen and H.B. Van Duzer appraise the estate of George Rae's deceased wife, Lottie. George Thatcher, Johan Poulsen and H. B. Van Duzer later act as executors for Robert Inman's estate. Robert Inman testifies in court on behalf of George Rae's estate. Johan Poulsen loans fellow executives H.B. Van Duzer and George Thatcher $40,000 each, then a tremendous sum. Through business downturns and labor difficulties that stop many a firm, management enjoys a unified front.

The Inman-Poulsen Lumber Company's founders possess the triple blessings of knowledge, foresight and leadership. From this, a collective wisdom develops. Theirs is a company ethic, reinforced by each man's individual strengths. In "Mills And Markets-A History of the [P]acific Coast Lumber Industry to 1900," lumber historian Thomas R. Cox describes this most important factor:

*...it seems clear that those firms that prospered did so not just because they were the largest and financially soundest (in their early years they often were not), **but because of the quality of leadership they enjoyed.*** [Bold added].

Ample evidence shows Inman-Poulsen management enjoys quality leadership. And though each man has a different personality, the co-founders share much in common. Their hard work and good business instincts are guided with a sense of purpose. Prior to their forming Inman-Poulsen, the co-founders each ascend their own ladder of success. Recognizing the potential of their combined talents, the men figuratively connect their individual ladders end-to-end, taking them all to dizzying heights. From their earliest days, the men sense great opportunity, not obstacles.

The story of Inman-Poulsen is a case study of what teamwork can accomplish with effort and perseverance. Faith in their own problem-solving ability allows the firm to turn challenges into possibilities. This infectious 'can-do' attitude is to become a perpetual company trait.

As immigrants, the Scottish-born Rae and Scandinavian Poulsen share a common bond, for America is not their native land. Inman and Hatfield too, are also far from their Ohio beginnings. None of the men can count on nearby relatives to "pull strings" on their behalf, for all lack the benefit of such family connections to lighten their burden. The co-founder's experiences are compelling, their lives interwoven within the fabric of Oregon history.

Robert David Inman

...there was no man in Portland or in the state of Oregon, who was more universally respected than Robert D. Inman...His motto has been 'honesty and fairness to all...

History of Oregon III

Episodes in Robert Inman's life offer a window into the life of his business partners like George Rae. Rae leaves no known diary or journal, yet people are frequently understood through their associations. As a result, insight about George Rae is garnered through business relationships with his co-founders. It's telling that Rae works with Robert Inman, who habitually thinks big.

As I study Inman's life, it's difficult not to be impressed. Newspapers of the time conjure many adjectives to describe his greatness. Inman's life begins in the small town of Piqua, Ohio. While his American lineage traces back to the revolutionary war, he has anything but an easy life, especially as a child. Robert Inman's Yankee father dies fighting in the Civil War at the battle of Shiloh under General Ulysses S. Grant April 6-7, 1862.

Family circumstances are so dire, Robert works before the age of 10 as a towboy in the old Ohio Canal. Looking for an honest job to support his widowed mother, he then begins work in a sawmill. The abilities of this mechanic's son fulfill a family trait. His mother cannot provide for her young boy.

Robert agrees to voluntary servitude in order to pay his way west. In 1865 at the age of 12, R. D. Inman joins a wagon train of emigrants bound for the Pacific Coast. The following few pages from one of Inman's speeches read like an adventure novel and provide insight to the beginnings of this future timber pioneer.

On the 21st day of May, 1865...we went along about a quarter of a mile from where we were camped and I soon discovered we were going to one of those so-called 'neck-tie parties.' My recollection is that it was conducted by what was called a vigilance committee. The criminal had robbed a man of five dollars a few days before. Being a boy of 12 years, just the right age to take in and remember most everything, I naturally had the whole affair so imprinted on my mind that it seems but yesterday.

They brought the poor devil out of a little improvised jail and led him under a green willow tree and then tied his hands behind him, put a dry goods box under him, tied a piece of bed cord around his neck, fastened it to a limb of the tree, kicked the box from under him and then ordered everybody away. That was my first practical knowledge of stern justice dealing with wrong-doers.

Later in his narrative, Inman adds:

We then crossed the Missouri and continued our journey westward until we came to a ferry on the Platte River. We camped there on the banks of the river about a week, and such sport as the men had, hunting and fishing. It certainly would make a sportsman of today green with envy-antelope, deer, bear, wolves and coyotes galore.

We finally got across the river by ferrying the wagons and swimming across. The prices charged by the ferrymen were so high that the men would not pay the price, and that is why the stock were made to swim across instead of being ferried...through treacherous quicksands and ugly currents of that old river. Thanks to the watchfulness and skill of a young athletic fellow by the name of Bittner, I was pulled out and rolled over a keg until the muddy water I had taken in was pretty well out of me and I was soon all right again, getting only a good lecture from the old ma, Mr. Davidson, for my foolhardiness.

At this point, Inman mentions attaching a biting fish called 'gar' to one steer's backside. The animals spook so

badly, it takes three days to round them up. Later in his
speech, he continues:

> *The next resting place I remember was a place*
> *called Green [M]eadow. Here again we laid over for rest.*
> *Mr. Davidson lost two of his horses here by their eating some*
> *poisonous weed, and the water was so impregnated with*
> *alkali that soda had to be mixed with it to neutralize the*
> *effect of the poison on the stock. By this time we had learned*
> *the value of buffalo chips, as that was about the only fuel we*
> *had, as there was very little timber of any kind...Here we*
> *were joined by more wagons, so when we pulled out again*
> *there were sixty-nine wagons in our train. Here also*
> *firearms were put in shape as we were beginning to hear*
> *quite a bit of talk about hostile Indians.*

Inman recounts more 'prairie justice' later in the
journey:

> *There was an old German who belonged to another*
> *train camped near our train. One night two of his mules, a*
> *very fine pair, was stolen. They caught the two thieves and*
> *brought them back and held a council about what to do with*
> *them. After deliberating awhile they decided that the thieves*
> *must die. They gave them their choice either to be hanged or*
> *shot. They chose the former.*

Inman proceeds to detail the pioneer caravan's
encounters with danger:

> *We were now in Wyoming, passing Fort Laramie, a*
> *little military post. We had traveled some ten hundred miles*
> *by this time. I was riding along behind the herd about 3 p.m.*
> *when the first thing I knew I heard the most unearthly yell*
> *imaginable. I began to look around and to my horror I could*
> *see Indians in almost every direction. They were all mounted*

and seemed to be circling around the train. Most of them were armed with bows, arrows and long spears, although some of them had firearms. It is marvelous how expert they were with their bows and arrows. Our train was in rather bad shape for the attack, as they were scattered over a mile or more of the road, but the captain got to work quickly to have the train formed into a corral.

In the meantime I was still trying with my lazy pony to get the loose stock to the train, but the first thing I knew along came an Indian on horseback riding like the wind. He did not seem to be over thirty or forty yards from me. I could see the painted stripes on his face quite plainly. He let fly two or three arrows at me, but luckily for me he was riding very fast and his aim was poor. I was not hit, but one of the arrows went so close in front of me that I felt the wind from it in my face and heard its whirr as it went past me.

By this time I concluded it was time for me to make for tall timber, so headed my pony for the train. I did not look back till I reached [the] train. I do not know just why this Indian did not take me in, as it would have been an easy matter for him to have overhauled me and ran me through with his spear. I got to the train safe and sound, but [was] about the most scared boy you ever saw.

Inman's narrative next takes on an especially serious tone to describe the traveling caravan's casualties. The experience is recalled forty years after the event and describes capture and murder of pioneers on the way West. Inman then describes the final leg of their journey.

The train had by this time decreased to six or eight wagons, as they kept dropping out to wend their way to their final destination The following morning we rolled our wagon on the steamboat at The Dalles and on the evening of

November 1st arrived in Portland, which had a population then of about 3,000. We were just five months and eleven days making the journey, and the first time I went back to the starting place the trip was made in three days. There certainly was quite a contrast between the speed of the old 'prairie schooner' and the modern 'iron horse.'

Inman's detailed recollection—decades later—illustrates the westward journey's lasting impact on those who survive. In suffering severe hardship and witnessing death, R. D. Inman develops a perspective that later helps him to overcome difficulties not nearly so dangerous. Compared to dodging arrows, success in the competitive lumber business must have seemed tame.

Many jobs follow for R. D. Inman. Farmhand, tie-cutter, railroad brakeman, fireman and circus worker. Inman is later hired at the Willamette Steam Saw Mills in 1868, piling lumber. When he begins, Inman is not expected to last longer than the other workers, who usually quit or are soon fired.

Before long, Inman is promoted to the machinist department. He learns different positions in the mill and acquires a knack for fixing broken machinery. This makes Inman valuable to have around and endears him to his employer. After seven years at Willamette Steam Saw Mills, he helps organize the North Pacific Lumber Company. Garnering one-fourth ownership of that firm, he oversees construction of their new mill. This added experience in lumber company development and mill construction gives Inman excellent preparation for what lies ahead.

In 1889, Robert Inman resigns his position and sells his interest in the North Pacific Lumber Company. This frees him to devote attention to his new challenge, the Inman-Poulsen Lumber Company. Later in his career, Inman works to bring manufacturing firms to Portland and founds the business organization that later becomes Associated Oregon Industries. Inman is also recognized as a peace-maker in business circles. One report notes his address to fellow members of the colorful woodmen's fraternity called Hoo-Hoo's:

[Inman] stated that the organization tended to bring men in kindred lines closer together. The idea that a competitor was our natural born enemy was a mistake. When you come to rub up against him you generally find he is a pretty good fellow. The trouble with most business men is that they give too little attention to the social side of life, and as a result, their best traits are undeveloped in the mad rush of business cares.

Inman then heartily endorses his favorite club:

Hoo Hoo is essentially a strong social order. I belong to a good many orders, but feel and think I express the opinion of many others, that for a real good time Hoo Hoo beats them all.

Carey's "History of Oregon" validates the character of Inman-Poulsen Lumber's senior partner:

In spite of the disadvantages of youth and without the assistance of influential friends he has risen to a position of affluence. Riding a western-bound wagon train from Ohio, he fought Indians and witnessed much bloodshed. A staunch Democrat, in 1892, Inman was elected to the state legislature and the first Multnomah County Democrat elected in 20 years. Appointed chairman of the Port of Portland Commission assisting in the plans for permanent port construction.

In 1900, Inman was elected to state senate on the Citizens ticket. Unlike many, he resigned his seat when nominated for mayor of Portland (he was defeated). In addition to all these posts, Inman found time to serve as water commissioner, was a member of the Board of Trade, President, Oregon Automobile Club, Chamber of Commerce, the Portland Rowing Club, the Commercial Club, Multnomah Athletic Club and served on a bank's board of directors.

Johan Poulsen

    Johan Poulsen's reputation as a level-headed accountant is a good match for R. D. Inman's mechanical genius. Poulsen is born in the once-Danish region of Schleswig, now part of northern Germany. He immigrates to the United States as a young man. Like other Inman-Poulsen co-founders, Poulsen's industriousness helps define his character.

    Poulsen is involved in several startup timber firms while managing Inman-Poulsen. After co-founding Inman-Poulsen in 1890, he co-founds the Oregon Pine Lumber Company in 1895.

In 1902 he teams with several lesser-known lumber executives to form yet another firm, the City Retail Lumber Company, with the stated intent to "...sell and deal in lumber and building material." This big, bookish man with an affinity for precious jewels keeps many irons in the fire.

Financial whiz Johan Poulsen dies October 29, 1929. Ironically, it's also a day known throughout the world as 'Black Tuesday,' the very date a cataclysmic stock market crash triggers the Great Depression. Johan Poulsen leaves an estate then valued at slightly less than $200,000. Most Portland residents are familiar with the Queen Anne style home he built, located at the east end of Portland's Ross Island bridge. Road changes have since altered its surroundings. Inman-Poulsen co-founder Robert Inman also had a matching home built nearby and the two imposing mansions stood for many years. Inman's home was destroyed in 1956 to make way for road improvements.

Job Hatfield

Of all the Inman-Poulsen co-founders, Job Hatfield keeps perhaps the lowest profile. A devoted family man, the native Ohioan is born in 1855. Hatfield is educated at the National Normal School Teacher's Department in Lebanon, Ohio. He's a good student and receives his certificate in 1879. Job Hatfield travels to Oregon and in 1882, marries George and Lottie Rae's oldest daughter Edna, with her parents in attendance.

Eight years later, Hatfield and Rae are business partners and comprise management's unnamed half of the Inman-Poulsen Lumber Company. Job Hatfield works as a collector for the firm. The relationship between Job Hatfield and his father-in-law appears to have been friendly, but not informal. Correspondence with his wife Edna, George Rae's daughter, reveals that even after knowing him for years, Job Hatfield politely refers to his father-in-law as "Mr. Rae."

Job & Edna Hatfield

By 1897, Job Hatfield is working for the newly-formed Oregon Pine Lumber Company. In 1899, Hatfield rejoins Inman-Poulsen. Why, with so many mouths to feed does Hatfield wander from an envied firm like Inman-Poulsen for the uncertainty of a startup company? The mystery is solved in realizing fellow Inman-Poulsen co-founder Johan Poulsen co-founds Oregon Pine Lumber Company as president in 1895.

What kind of a man is Job Hatfield? A courteous one, as seen through the eyes of his associates. Hatfield is esteemed by respectable men. It's also significant that he enjoys an alliance with giants of industry in his mid-thirties.

Most compelling are letters between Job Hatfield and his family during his travels in California. Hatfield sends at least three letters to his wife and daughters on one particular trip. Hatfield also receives at least two letters while there, one from his wife Edna and another from his daughter Minnie, then 13 years old. Written between June 24 and July 5th, 1900, it is the last known correspondence between Job Hatfield and his family.

Hatfield's letters provide a flavor of the times. They address topics like how Hatfield arrived in California (on the steamer Columbia, from Portland to San Francisco), where he stays (the Grand Hotel in San Francisco and the Paso Robles Hotel in Paso Robles) along with other insightful details about daily experiences in California during the year 1900.

But with a wife and five daughters back in Portland, Oregon, what exactly is Hatfield doing far away in California? Records indicate he makes a courtesy call to a nearby Inman-Poulsen outpost. Yet it's faltering health that has Hatfield visiting the purported healing waters of Paso Robles.

Paso Robles Cal. July 5, 1900

     ...I am getting along as well as I can expect in such a short time. I haven't been here long enough to tell how my dissyness [sic] is going to do. I know my stomach is much better. The doctor told me to go down to the spring and drink [two] glasses of hot sulphur water one hour before each meal. I went down yesterday morning at 6AM and drank two glasses...I told the doctor if I drank any more of that warm water it would run me to death...

> *Job Hatfield*
> *Spring Hotel*
> *Paso Robles*

     Three days later, 45 year old Job Hatfield is dead. The Saturday, July 14, 1900 edition of California's Paso Robles Record acknowledges Hatfield and his success in a brief obituary.

Death of Job Hatfield

The death of J. Hatfield of Portland, Oregon occurred at the Paso Robles Hotel last Sunday. Heart failure was the direct cause of his demise. The body was taken to the undertaking parlors of J. E. Burket and there embalmed and shipped to Portland. The deceased was a wealthy lumberman of Oregon. A wife and several children survive him.

Given Hatfield's means and surviving children, it is significant that he dies intestate. This is not the case with his fellow co-founders Inman, Poulsen or Rae. The reason Hatfield has no written will is possibly due to his young age. Job Hatfield's estate is eventually settled in Multnomah County court. Surviving is Hatfield's 34 year old widow, Edna, along with 5 daughters, aged 2 months to 17 years.

True to the strong bond among Inman-Poulsen's co-founders, Poulsen and Rae act as appraisers of Hatfield's estate, whose Inman-Poulsen stock they value at $7,500. Upon his death, Hatfield's wealth—including company stock—is valued at just under $14,000.

While not a king's ransom in comparison to the other co-founders, it is then a princely sum. Perspective of Hatfield's wealth in relative terms can be grasped by comparing his estate with the value of a typical house at the time. The average price of a home in the year of Hatfield's death is then approximately $5,000.

Inman, Poulsen and Rae live considerably longer than Job Hatfield and their firm enjoys strong growth in the years to follow. With their prime earning years still ahead, the remaining co-founders have time to amass substantial wealth. Also in their favor are no business or income taxes throughout the first part of the 20th century to slow them down.

A Big Break

By now, I've reviewed dozens of independent sources on George Rae and many who know him. Finding unmined information is difficult. I pore over each file anew. Given the often formal writing style of the time, I search for shades of subtlety and nuance, trying to detect variations in focus, prose and tone. But there's only so much I can wring from each shred of remaining evidence.

In some ways, I feel no closer to solving nagging riddles that epitomize George Rae's life. Big questions, like what made him 'tick,' and simple curiosity—like just how thick was his Scottish brogue? I've found some interesting information so far, but something tells me there's more to uncover. The downside appearing negligible, I continue, only to turn up the same tired sources. Before digging any deeper into what is now an obsession, I resolve to find fresh ground.

Considering my next move, I ponder: How about finding more about his second wife, the woman lying in state next to him? Afraid to get my hopes up, I remind myself that *so little* is known about Elizabeth Rae. Besides, I've tried before. Even the Multnomah County Library, among my best sources, doesn't have much more to offer about her.

As a result, each time I consider the possibility of learning more about Elizabeth, I predictably drift back to the lumber baron. Yet it seems my options are to either focus on someone other than George Rae in the hope of locating at least a few more peripheral pieces to the puzzle of his life, or give up. But why *not* the baroness? Yet, with only a tiny obituary, where to look? Unproductive genealogy inquiries and fruitless Internet searches spark a quest to find public documents on Elizabeth. If any exist, they're over half a century old.

In time, I finally ask my amateur legal mind the one question that could help break this information log jam. How about the probate index? By now, I'm fuzzy on what might possibly be found at the Multnomah County courthouse. But given my hours reviewing an incredible number of old documents, I'm heartened to know it won't be a problem to work the courthouse microfilm machines. Lunch hour at the Multnomah County Courthouse is well spent, because I locate what I came for: The estate file on Elizabeth Rae.

Records on her were right here—after all this time. Page after page of documents reveal that Elizabeth shares the wealth. Upon her death in 1942, she wills gifts to a few dozen loved ones. Although I can appreciate her magnanimity, what I'd give for a bit of background, or an interesting anecdote. Wishing I'd thought of looking for information about Elizabeth Rae at the courthouse sooner, it encourages me to keep going. After so many years, the prospect of finding relatives familiar with Elizabeth is dicey. I try anyway. Alas, no current names in various directories around Portland, Oregon appear to match those on her will. Rechecking the estate's beneficiaries, I realize their ages now approach the century mark.

One Sunday afternoon on a lark, I phone an out-of-state household sharing the same last name and city address on my dwindling list of Elizabeth's relatives from court documents. Clara Dubbs of Ransom, Kansas answers the phone. She's very pleasant with a slight mid-western accent. We talk a while before I ask about her distant relative entombed next to a lumber baron. Her memory is clear: "...We'd always heard she married a millionaire. I didn't know her, but was always told she married well."

But one thing is certain. A young Illinois-born Elizabeth makes her way west and lands in Portland. Beyond that, details are sketchy. She is said to have managed a boarding house somewhere along the way. Clara kindly sends me a postcard, and mentions that her cousin Melba Tillitson, apparently a great-niece of Elizabeth, has several pictures of her great-aunt. I place the postcard in a safe place and begin working on some other leads.

One afternoon while on my computer, I notice an unfamiliar e-mail address with a file attached. It's from the Tillitson family. As the file downloads, the image before me is revealed to be Elizabeth. Ever since I first entered the Rae Room, I wondered what Elizabeth looked like. Now I know. The photo ushers forth her humanity, bringing Elizabeth to life once more. It also forever replaces my only other image of her—a name on a cold stone tomb.

Born while Ulysses S. Grant is president, Elizabeth is no longer an imaginary being to me. Now having seen her face, her existence is very real. Included with the photo are several others. Each reveals a tall, poised woman. Her seemingly calm demeanor will become even more remarkable as her life unfolds before me. As I receive additional documents, a clearer picture appears of Elizabeth Rae.

George Rae & Inman-Poulsen

George Rae's name is conspicuously absent from the handwritten document that incorporates Inman-Poulsen Lumber Company in 1890. Yet, multiple contemporaneous sources name Rae as a co-founder and Vice-President. On day one of their new company, Inman, Poulsen and Job Hatfield are signatories. Their timber troika soon makes way for Rae. On company letterhead barely a year after the firm is founded, George Rae's name is found below those of Inman and Poulsen, yet above Job Hatfield.

Rae's job history reads like a Horatio Alger resume. His lumber beginnings are low key, but records document a deliberate ascent. Like other Inman-Poulsen co-founders, he first has jobs with different sawmill companies. After years working for Portland's Willamette Steam Mills and the North Pacific Lumber Company, Rae's resume' includes positions as mill hand, timekeeper, and yard foreman. Judging by his steady upward climb, Rae's abilities are recognized early.

1890 begins a new era for each Inman-Poulsen co-founder. So pivotal is this year, that it segments the men's lives with the neatness of a new saw blade. It's as if their existence could be partitioned "Life Before 1890" and "Life After 1890." This is because they form the business that is to be their crowning achievement precisely one decade before the 20th Century dawns.

Inman-Poulsen's co-founders can not possibly know what to expect. Yet they recognize each other's unique strengths and decide to enter the future together. While Inman-Poulsen's co-founders possess different talents and temperaments, they share a common work ethic. The Inman-Poulsen team is overflowing with the stuff of success, even before they achieve wealth. R.D. Inman, master mechanic. Johan Poulsen, accounting wizard. Job Hatfield, trustworthy collector of funds. George Rae, salesman par excellence.

Affiliations afford the once blue-collar Rae entrée to another world. His status growing, George Rae acquires added polish through diverse contacts and memberships. Shattering the bonds of his native land's class structure, Rae's investment in social enhancement becomes a practical course of education and pays dividends. Before long, this son of a manure merchant is an executive with a successful firm and recognized as a professional. His influence expands with his business connections.

Rae's memberships in traditional fraternal orders of the day grow. He joins popular groups like the Elks, Masons, Shriners and the Lang Syne Society (a businessman's club). They grant Rae cachet among Portland's executive class. One can only assume that his native accent lends authenticity to every Scottish Rite meeting he attends. Yet Rae moves at his own pace. While business partner Robert Inman is a longtime member and officer of the jovial, loose-knit group of competing timber executives called Hoo-Hoo's, Rae doesn't formally join that order until August 8, 1903.

Chapter VII: A New World Record

Portland, Oregon's lumber reputation is solidified with the June 4, 1905 publication of the Sunday Oregonian. The headline story trumpets "Great Lumber City." About one year later, rare words from George Rae are found in the Oregonian's June 2, 1906 edition. That headline precedes details of the firm's awesome achievement:

BREAKS LUMBER RECORD
IMMENSE OUTPUT FROM INMAN-POULSEN
MILL DURING MAY

Concern Sawed Over 13,000,000 Feet of Lumber During Month. 'Frisco Demand the Cause

With the avowed intention of breaking the world's record for a month's output of lumber, the Inman-Poulsen Lumber Company kept its plant in operation 22 hours out of each 24 during the month of May, and how well it succeeded in accomplishing the object is shown by the product of the plant which turned out 13,300,000 feet of lumber from May 1 to May 31.

Vice-President George Rae, of the Inman-Poulsen Company, stated that in his opinion the record established by his company during the past month would not be equalled by any single mill in the United States, or in fact, in the world.

Inman-Poulsen Lumber Company has incentive to perform at such high capacity. The San Francisco earthquake of April 18, 1906 is a tremendous blow to many Californians, but a windfall for Inman-Poulsen. The disaster spurs lumber demand among West Coast sawmills. The need for lumber to rebuild San Francisco has much to do with the record set by the Inman-Poulsen mill. In order to accommodate the enormous orders received, it is necessary to work both day and night shifts overtime.

During this era profitable for companies like Inman-Poulsen, labor unions gain the ear of hard-working employees. Inman-Poulsen is not immune to management-union squabbles. In a time of union-friendly "Wobblies," striking workers begin to find their voice.

Yet, Inman-Poulsen executives are not exactly robber-barons of yore. With labor-friendly Robert Inman at the helm, Inman-Poulsen provides living-wage jobs to thousands over the decades. Inman-Poulsen competes "head to head" for good workers against other companies and thrives at the challenge.

Inman-Poulsen's co-founders are amply compensated for their years of effort and now enjoy the best life has to offer. Rewarded with prosperity, their surfeit is staggering. It includes mansions, the finest food, fashionable clothes and high class transportation. In the days before automobiles, Portland residents witness the executives and their wives as they tour the city, first in horse and carriage and later in automobiles.

Lottie Rae in an undated photo. Note dog and buggy whip.

Life After Lumber

After a record year in 1906, George Rae reduces his involvement in the lumber trade at a time when business could hardly be better. Rae retains his association with Inman-Poulsen and whether fortuitous or planned, both his entrance and gradual exit from the timber trade is expertly timed. He is not alone.

Wealthy Oregon lumber executive George Weidler also reduces his industry holdings. During the landmark production year of 1906, renowned Northwest lumberman John Yeon sells his timber interests, then buys the first of his major Portland properties. Yeon later associates with timber magnate Simon Benson in the hotel business.

In 1907, Norwegian-born Benson is considered Portland's wealthiest lumber man. Benson (Polytechnic) High School and the Benson Hotel are both named after him. Benson sells his lumber stake in 1910 for over 4 million dollars, then purchases what is to become his million dollar Benson Hotel in 1913. This successful businessman is remembered for both his hotel and the many "Benson fountains" around Portland. To discourage alcohol consumption, Benson commissions the drinking fountains still in use today.

It's noteworthy that numerous wealthy Oregon lumbermen envision a sea change in their business around the same time and opt to pursue new opportunities. With decades of the trade under his suspenders, George Rae is familiar with good and lean years. As signs of a lumber slowdown approach Portland's horizon, Rae's focus has shifted. Buoyed by success, in 1906 George Rae builds a new home in the Colonial Heights neighborhood of Southeast Portland.

Relative Difficulty

Initially, few details turn up on Maud Rae, the adopted daughter of George & Lottie Rae. Two decades younger than the Rae's other daughter Edna, young Maud is, as her own attorney later admits, "rather wild." Court records reveal Maud's Protestant parents send her to Sacred Heart Academy, a Catholic school located on what was known as "Piety Hill" in Salem, Oregon. But once more, my mine of information appears tapped out.

I stroll countless aisles through the Multnomah County library, local bookstores, anywhere—hoping to better understand the Rae story. I scour books from the time on lumber history, timber management, everything. Now bolstered by my repeated ability to reverse out of what often appears to be a dead end, I think things through once more. "Portland is the town the Rae's called home," I reason. "What other information might still be found?" Answers beckon at a different place.

Eventually I discover a rich vein of material to be mined at the Oregon Historical Society's library in downtown Portland. I'm so impressed with their wealth of material, I eventually become a member. One evening while researching photo files there, I happen upon a most surprising find. It is an image of young Maud Rae around 1909. At about the time when the photo was taken, George Rae's wife Lottie is exhibiting symptoms of severe mental illness.

On October 12, 1908, George Rae formally asks to be named as her legal guardian. Rae's petition before the court states "...Lottie Rae has been for more than a year...of weak and unsound mind and incapable of taking care of herself and her property."

Two days later, Lottie Rae is petitioned to appear in a court hearing on October 27th, 1908 for the purpose of determining her mental capacity. It doesn't go well. Less than a week later, Lottie Rae is declared insane. In February 1909, the court designates George Rae as his wife's guardian. After spending considerable time in several private sanitariums, Lottie is eventually committed to the Oregon State Insane Asylum in nearby Salem, Oregon. His wife incapacitated, Rae next plays matchmaker for his young unmarried daughter. Before long, a male suitor is found.

31 year old Theodore Seth (T.S.) Emerson is the strong-willed son of a wealthy Seattle produce broker. With George Rae's prompting and his maid Elizabeth as a witness, Rae's daughter Maud becomes Mrs. T.S. Emerson on August 20, 1912. As the vows are spoken, Maud doesn't know someone in her own wedding party will soon hold sway over

her wealthy father's estate. The fuse has been lit for a bombshell. But, I am to learn, that's not all. For T.S. Emerson, the Rae clan's latest member—and Maud's new husband—has his own plans as well. Eventually, enmity sown between young T.S. Emerson and George Rae exposes particularly ignoble motives.

Chapter VIII: The Long Goodbye

Professional success is no antidote for the personal trials that beset George Rae. He amasses power and a mighty fortune, yet Rae's influence over the foreboding shadow of his wife's mental condition is meager. Lottie Rae is infirmed in mental hospitals for the better part of a decade. Initially committed to a private Portland institution in 1908, over time her condition worsens. In 1911, she is transferred to the Oregon State Sanitarium—founded in 1883 and now famous as the setting for the film 'One Flew Over The Cuckoo's Nest.'

During this time, George Rae is dealt what some might call an especially bad hand in the poker game of life. Given such tragedy, otherwise solid souls can turn rudderless and drift into obscurity. Others, faith shaken, seek solace in self-pity. But deep within George Rae is the strength to go on. It's as if his pain is vanquished with Goethe's maxim: 'That which does not kill me makes me stronger.' George Rae finds relief from his depressing situation with travel. Time away provides relief from his load of family concerns, including difficulties with adopted daughter Maud and Lottie's losing battle with mental illness.

Catalina Escape

One of the photos I eventually receive from Melba Tillitson places Elizabeth, George Rae's then-maid, in a sportsman's environment 26 miles off the California coast at Catalina Island in December, 1912. Looking at the photo, I feel uncertain Elizabeth would travel alone and clear to another state for a fishing trip. Literally, at least, George Rae is not in the picture.

Catalina Island has long enjoyed a reputation as a

pleasant vacation spot. It also has a history of celebrity. Upon receiving the photo of Elizabeth Rae, I search for and find a contemporaneous description of Catalina Island in author Charles Frederick Holder's guide, 'The Channel Islands of California.' Holder deftly paints an idyllic port town where people and nature co-exist:

Avalon possesses a charm that sooner or later involves the visitor who has a love of nature in his makeup....[At Catalina]...a grove of stately eucalyptus trees...shelter the homes of eight or nine thousand people in summer, and of many all the year around. The town climbs the hills and canons...

The island is also a wealth magnet. Early in the 20th century around the time Elizabeth visits, Catalina Island is a retreat for the Wrigley's of chewing gum fame, plus legendary Hollywood entertainers like Charlie Chaplin and Laurel & Hardy. Three boats a day arrive at Catalina from Los Angeles. Given toney accoutrements and a lifestyle geared to moneyed seafarers, Catalina Island is a haven for the well-heeled. Activities at this marine mecca include horseback riding, golf, shooting, tennis and yachting. But Holder's book leaves little doubt about Catalina's main draw:

The bay is filled with launches and boats of all kinds, devoted to this sport. There is a fleet of glass-bottomed boats; fleets of rowboats and yachts of the owners who live on the slopes of the neighboring hills over looking the bay. Avalon is a remarkable town, inasmuch as it is based on angling with rod and reel. Here yearly is held the greatest convocation of sea-anglers in the world, as they come from everywhere. There are varied allurements, such as the climate and pastimes, but the one thing upon which Avalon is based is the fishing, and everything is subservient to that.

Elizabeth Rae with man identified as Captain George Bosch.
My catch at Catalina Island California, December 21ˢᵗ, 1912.

Holder describes a scene much like what Elizabeth
experiences first-hand. It even details the place where her
day's catch of fish is likely viewed and weighed in a photo:

*The angling interest becomes acute at the south side
of the bay, where a long pier leads out into the water—a
structure absolutely unique. It is the resort of the
professional tuna boatmen. At the end of this angling pier
are two singular objects. One looks like a gallows, another
is a locked scale. On the first, the great game fish—of from
twenty to five hundred pounds—are weighed and
photographed. In the morning, at noon and at night this pier
is the centre of attraction, as all the fish taken in the
tournaments must come in here to be weighed...*

Elizabeth's nice catch of fish speaks for itself.
Identifiable in the photo are tuna and even a small shark

hanging above and behind the captain. George Rae likely stands next to the photographer, lest a scandalous photo with his maid in a faraway place catch the attention of wags. George is still married to Charlotte while Elizabeth accompanies him on such excursions, including Europe. These trips later cause much trouble. In another document I receive, Elizabeth's message to family members on the back of an envelope dated March 3, 1913 reads:

Am having a fine time. I leave this P.M. for Cuba. Will return in ten days or two weeks then go to Wash DC. EEM [Elizabeth Emma Maxwell]

Throughout this time, Lottie Rae is being held at the state mental hospital in Salem, Oregon. Curious about the place, I wonder whether any records may still exist about Lottie Rae. Eventually I decide to pay a visit to the records office at the Oregon State Hospital's mental health division.

I approach the hospital and observe institutional looking grounds with a campus-like feel. Entering the old main building, I have an odd sense of what it might have been like nearly 100 years earlier when Lottie is a patient. And though I'm more than six feet tall, the corridors seem imposing. I can only imagine how a frail and frightened Lottie might have felt. Two office workers study me as I open a hall door and enter their domain. "Hi, I'm looking for records on a former patient early in the 20th century. Is this the right place?" They look at each other, then assure me it is.

While there, I complete a requisition form and a few weeks later, receive an official-looking letter from the Oregon Department of Human Resources. The return address is marked 'Medical Records.' I open it and am suddenly privy to long-confidential pages, each chock-full with details of Charlotte Rae's final tragic years. Each sheet is stamped with a confidentiality warning in bright red ink.

CONFIDENTIAL: This information has been disclosed to you from records whose confidentiality is protected by state and federal law...You are prohibited from making any further disclosure of this information without the specific written consent of the person to whom it pertains, or as otherwise permitted by these laws and regulations.

Without violating medical record confidentiality statutes, let's just say that I learn a great deal about the last years of Charlotte Rae's life. This insightful medical information also confirms that life in an early 20th century insane asylum can be a particularly unpleasant experience.

The final page in her life's most arduous chapter is written on an unseasonably mild winter evening. Lottie Rae loses her battle with illness and passes away in Salem, Oregon on January 12, 1914. Several days later, Lottie Rae is laid to rest at Portland's Riverview Cemetery in one of the family plots George Rae and his daughter Edna purchase 14 years earlier. Beside Lottie is an empty burial space reserved for her George. But that is not for now, and even then, not for long.

Chapter IX: The Love Story

Now a widower, George Rae waits nearly a year
before he formally commits to a future with Elizabeth. Hope
rekindled, he is ready to embark on a new adventure in his
already storied life. I find a short account of George &
Elizabeth's union in an issue of The Timberman dated
November, 1914. Yet the three-sentence announcement in a
regional lumber journal omits what presages their union—or
the tumult to follow:

> George Rae, aged 71, a member of the firm of
> the Inman-Poulsen Lumber Co., and Elizabeth
> E. Maxwell, aged 45, of Tenth and Salmon
> streets, were married in the royal suite of the
> Hotel Multnomah on November 6, in Portland
> Ore., by Rev. F.H. Hayes of Sellwood
> [B]aptist church. A wedding supper, with
> covers for 25, followed. After a wedding trip
> to California, Mr. And Mrs. Rae will make
> their home in Portland.

At first glance, the wedding date chosen seems odd.
That's because after years of friendship with George Rae, his
new bride Elizabeth is denied a traditional June wedding.
Neither will it occur amid bursts of sunshine, lush with the
promise blossoms bring. Even more puzzling, instead of a
Spring rite, an especially rainy season is selected for the
nuptials. Nor will they celebrate among evergreens in the
forest setting George finds so familiar. The lumber executive
and his new bride hold the glorious event indoors—during a
season famed for short days and wet weather.

Is George Rae uncaring, unthinking, or merely
impulsive? Actually, he has good reason to select this
seemingly inauspicious time to pledge himself to the woman
he loves, for November 6th is Elizabeth's birthday.

Marrying her in the royal suite of Portland's grand
Multnomah Hotel is a special gift on his bride's special day.

Then barely two years old, the Multnomah Hotel is
already a Portland landmark for major events. Through the
decades, it hosts luminaries like aviator Charles Lindbergh,
actress Mary Pickford, Queen Marie of Romania and Elvis
Presley. For many years the Multnomah is considered one of
the finer West Coast hotels.

Working as vice president overseeing sales at a top
lumber firm means George Rae manages a virtually all-male
workforce in a tough and grimy industry. During this era,
classic male behavior precludes pronouncement of deep
emotions. As a result, Rae's feelings for Elizabeth are, as
expected, little-chronicled. George Rae is not known for
poetic utterances. He is a businessman and a man of action.
So it's unrealistic to consider Rae at ease articulating his
closely-held thoughts with the facility of one familiar with
sentiment's exposition. George Rae shows affection more by
what he does.

While records show he gives alternate reasons for
matrimony, Rae's actions do the talking as he weds Elizabeth
in lavish style. Studying his behavior, there is little doubt of
George Rae's feelings for his new bride. As might be
expected, the lengthy illness of his first wife Lottie and her
subsequent death are wounds Rae may reasonably hope to
heal. With advanced age, eroding health and a strained
relationship with his daughter Maud, it's easy to imagine
Rae's hope is renewed in a new life with Elizabeth.

The lumber baron and his bride celebrate their new
life together in style. Others may later discount George
Rae's feelings toward Elizabeth for their own purposes. Yet
his actions are exquisitely-planned. He behaves deliberately
and boldly, as when he first set foot on a ship bound for the

United States forty five years earlier. George Rae is more than the craggy lumber baron seen in what few portraits remain. Whether Elizabeth wears high heels in their only known photo together is not known—she towers over him. No matter. To Elizabeth Rae, the stout, stern and stoop-shouldered man with rugged hands stands tallest of all.

Only known photo of George & Elizabeth Rae, circa 1914.

George Rae Is Laid To Rest

Less than four years after marrying Elizabeth Maxwell, George Rae passes away on February 12, 1918. The cause of death is labeled as kidney disease. A maelstrom develops shortly after his death. The source of contention? Rae's last will and testament, for it holds the key to his considerable wealth. But in reading his last wishes, one is struck by its utter clarity:

EXHIBIT A.

IN THE NAME OF GOD - - AMEN.

I, George Rae, being of sound and disposing mind and memory and being conscious of the frailty of human life, do make, publish and declare this my Last Will and Testament as follows, to wit:

FIRST: I hereby annul and revoke all and every Last Will and Testament heretofore made or executed by me, and declare this instrument to be my Last Will and Testament.

SECOND: I direct that my just debts and funeral expenses of last sickness be first paid out of my estate, and that I be buried with due regard to my station in life and the condition of my estate.

THIRD: I give, devise and bequeath to my beloved wife, Elizabeth E. Rae, of Portland, Oregon, thirty (30) shares of the capital stock of the Inman, Poulsen Lumber Company, an Oregon corporation, with its principal office and place of business at Portland, Multnomah County, Oregon.

FOURTH: I give, devise and bequeath to my nephew,

95

James Rae, of Harbor, Oregon, ten (10) shares of the capital stock of the corporation referred to in paragraph numbered three.

FIFTH: I give, devise and bequeath to my brother, William Rae, of Toronto, Canada, ten (10) shares of the capital stock of the corporation referred to in paragraph numbered three.

SIXTH: I give, devise and bequeath to Maud Rae, now Maud Emerson, an adopted daughter now living in Paris, France, the sum of Ten Dollars ($10.00) and direct that said sum be paid to her immediately upon the settlement of my estate.

SEVENTH: I hereby appoint Geo. W. Thatcher as the executor of this, my Last Will and Testament, and direct that he serve as such executor without being required to execute a bond therefor.

IN WITNESS WHEREOF, I have hereunto set my hand and seal this 9th day of December, 1914.

(Signed)   Geo. Rae,   (Seal)

The above instrument was at the date thereof signed, sealed, published and declared by the said George Rae as and for his Last Will and Testament in the presence of us, who at his request and in his presence and in the presence of each other, have subscribed our names as witnesses thereto.

George Rae's will is signed by witnesses Rosalia M. Hoffman and attorney William M. Cake.

Chapter X: War Over Fortune

There are distinct phases in the war for the Rae riches. Most involve court challenges from George Rae's adopted daughter Maud and her husband, T. S. Emerson. The legal paperwork keeps attorneys busy for years. After getting bogged down in legal minutiae more than once, I resolve to sift and determine the main issues.

There are two separate Rae battlefronts, though they get intertwined. One is a fight over Lottie Rae's estate. The other is for the estate of George Rae. Because of George's significant wealth, his estate is where things really heat up. But with help from their creative attorneys, Maud and T.S. Emerson relentlessly pursue both George and Lottie Rae's estates and take maximum advantage at each opportunity.

Round one in their court action against George Rae's estate starts with the accusation of Rae's improper accounting of his wife's finances. These alleged offenses occur between October 1908, when Lottie is declared insane, and September 1911, when she is committed to the state mental hospital in Salem.

Attorneys for T. S. and Maud Emerson take issue with George Rae's book-keeping methods. This is because George Rae pays his wife's private sanitarium expenses from her estate instead of his own. Thus, Maud and T.S. Emerson stand to inherit from an estate of Lottie's that is smaller, than if George Rae had paid her expenses out of his own funds. The Emerson legal team wins this round.

And rather than consent to the sale of a particular property in Lottie's estate, the Emerson legal team ascribes a 60% higher value, exhorting its use as a rental until the market improves. This claim is somewhat unusual, given the filing on behalf of Maud & T. S. Emerson after George and Lottie Rae are both deceased.

For this challenge, T. S. Emerson's father, businessman Horton S. Emerson travels from Seattle on behalf of his son & daughter-in-law to weigh in as Maud Rae Emerson's attorney-in-fact. One particular property is eventually sold to the Rae's other daughter, Edna Hatfield, for the original asking amount, at a price between tax-assessed and appraised values. While the Emerson legal team loses this particular skirmish, a protracted battle over George Rae's estate is already underway and the pace increases furiously.

Filing claim upon counter-claim, T. S. and Maud Emerson appear unconcerned about the expense and exhibit few compunctions about burning family bridges. Feverish legal maneuvering underscores their sense of entitlement and sheaves of litigation attest to a philosophy of winning at any cost. Round two of the Emerson-Rae bout follows after George Rae's adopted daughter Maud is essentially written out of his will in favor of Rae's second wife, Elizabeth.

Previous scuffles over Lottie Rae's estate are miniscule compared to the high stakes for George Rae's mammoth wealth. In round three, Maud and T. S. Emerson employ a 'scorched-earth' strategy. Tension on every conceivable legal issue builds between the parties, leading all the way to the Oregon Supreme Court.

Having found little information on T. S. Emerson, I decide to visit one of his former haunts, commonly known as "The Emerald City." It's a hot summer day when my wife Laurie joins me for the 3 1/2 hour car ride to Seattle. Laurie is helpful and by this time a bit hooked herself on this unfolding true-life drama. Our long drive ahead also gives us the opportunity to debate my latest theories and gain insight from a female perspective.

We stop at Seattle's famed Pike Street Market, have lunch and a do a little wandering. But our search for T. S. Emerson's former waterfront business location reveals few identifiable clues from so long ago. Next, we split up with our rendezvous pre-arranged. I hoof it east to the Seattle Public Library. My mission is simple. Find what I can about T. S. Emerson. Good questions come from knowing the home turf of George Rae's formidable opponent. Since any clues would be more than half a century old in a city I don't know well, I'll need all the help I can get.

The Seattle Public Library's main branch is massive. I soon realize if I'm to find information on T. S. Emerson, it won't be alone. I surrender and ask for assistance. An angel disguised as a librarian named Heather comes to my aid. I summarize the situation for her. "I'm looking for information about someone who lived in the area quite a while ago. I'm pretty sure he was a businessman."

While Heather listens intently, I sense my prospects are slim. With no promises, she directs me to an island of microfilm. Nearly an hour later, I'm opening my fourth pack of index reels in pursuit of a needle in this haystack of data. Just then, Heather walks up and simply asks "Is this him?" I stare at the evidence before me, the obituary of Theodore Seth Emerson. How she found it, I still don't know.

T. S. Emerson, Alaska Food Broker, Dies

T. S. Emerson, 62 years old, founder and owner of the Alaska Brokerage Company, died suddenly of a heart attack last night at his home, 2823 31st Ave. S.

Mr. Emerson was the son of the late H. S. Emerson,

pioneer Seattle produce broker. Born in Bismark, N. D., he came to Seattle many years ago, and in 1929 established the firm which since has handled a sizeable portion of the food and merchandise shipped to Alaska communities.

Mr. Emerson was known as a lover of music, and his home long has been a rendezvous for opera notables visiting Seattle. He is survived by his widow, Germane [sic] Emerson, and a daughter, Evelyn, both of Seattle. Funeral services will be held at 1 o'clock tomorrow in the Bonney-Watson chapel.

Though evening is fast approaching, I'm determined to see Emerson's former home before the long drive home. Now armed with an address and rejoined with my wife, I'm full of enthusiasm and promise. "Just 20 minutes, Honey and I know we'll find it." But as I eye T. S. Emerson's slim folder, part of me wonders if the home of this man still even exists. Will we find a vacant lot?

Steering our car with my left hand, my right hand points at several likely streets on the map between us. We take turns guessing the appearance of a property once owned by someone who, some ninety years earlier, butts heads so hard with George Rae. In a quiet neighborhood of old Seattle, we indeed find the former home of T. S. Emerson. The property is attractive, yet unpretentious by today's standards, especially to have once hosted luminaries of the opera. I snap a few photos before heading home and wonder what those gatherings must have been like.

Prelude To A War

Several attorneys represent George Rae's estate in court to defend the will's validity. Most visible among them is W. M. Cake, an experienced Inman-Poulsen Lumber

Company litigator. A principal of the law firm Cake & Cake with his brother Harry and later with Harry's son, Ralph, W. M. Cake is a personal signatory to Rae's will. So Cake is not just George Rae's attorney, but also a witness and virtual author of his will now before the court, to boot.

Rae Estate Attorney W.M. Cake

Both W. M. Cake and the will's other witness, Cake's secretary, Rosalia Hoffman, give depositions during the trial. They confirm that the will before the court is the same one they witness George Rae sign, and that Rae was "...of sound and disposing mind and not under any restraint or undue influence..." Cake is in the unique position to tell the court precisely what George Rae's instructions are. If anyone alive knows George Rae's precise intent for the handling of his estate, it is W. M. Cake, because he penned Rae's will.

Maud and T. S. Emerson retain A. C. Spencer and Edwin G. Amme as attorneys. In an interesting twist, both lawyers have ties to the opposition. A. C. Spencer once works at the same law office as his opponent, W. M. Cake. Attorney Edwin Amme is related by marriage to George Rae's grandchild, Eva Hatfield, daughter of Inman-Poulsen Lumber co-founder, Job Hatfield.

Appealing to the court's virtuous sensibilities, the Emerson team's strategy portrays George and Elizabeth's relationship as tawdry and their marriage a sham. They have ammunition for these assaults, given George and Elizabeth's travels both foreign and domestic prior to their marriage. Yet George Rae's will is damaging to the Emerson's case.

Emerson Attorney Edwin G. Amme

Attorneys for Maud and T. S. Emerson are experienced enough to know that if the case rests solely on that key document's legality, they will likely lose. So in a familiar legal maneuver, they place the focus squarely on Elizabeth's character in an attempt to expose her as a gold-digger. In tarnishing Elizabeth's reputation, their hoped outcome is to make her the unsympathetic recipient of questionably-received gain.

Upon learning the contents of George Rae's will, the Emerson team challenges it in Multnomah County Court. Portland's biggest newspapers break the Rae legal war and give it ample coverage in installments. In this age before television and the Internet, the local press presents the court proceedings with tabloid-like titillation.

Portland's newspapers serve each new morsel in salacious detail, providing a veritable feast to their readers. Ever-innovative, Emerson attorneys next bring a then-familiar, but controversial federal law into the fray. As a result, the fires of gossip soon turn white hot with The Oregon Daily Journal's coverage of the battle's next front.

Rae Is Forced To Wed Housekeeper, Declares Amme.

FEAR OF PROSECUTION UNDER MANN WHITE SLAVE ACT LED TO MARRIAGE, WITNESS TELLS COURT.

Citing the Mann Act is high courtroom drama and the Rae team scrambles. Named after that bill's chief proponent—Illinois legislator James Robert Mann—the 1910 law is originally established with the intent to protect young women from abduction across state lines for purposes of prostitution. Today it may seem unlikely that a man could face criminal charges for traveling with his forty-ish housekeeper. But given the tenor of the times, George Rae undertakes an element of risk in his travels with Elizabeth.

Emerson attorney Edwin Amme informs the court that George Rae once told Amme he married Elizabeth in fear she'd blackmail him with the Mann Act. But this approach is hardly airtight. That's because the Mann Act's raison d' etre is to prevent kidnapping and prostitution, not consensual travel. Yet to the Emerson team's advantage, the Mann Act is selectively enforced and unevenly prosecuted.

By 1917, three years after George and Elizabeth Rae marry, the Mann Act is effectively expanded to prevent non-commercial sex in the decision of *Caminetti v. United States.*

It's difficult to know if Rae clearly states he marries Elizabeth due to fear of the Mann Act, for it's an opposing attorney's memory against a deceased George Rae. Even if Rae speaks as accused, his actions shout otherwise. Another problem arises from the suggestion Rae is concerned at all with the Mann Act. That's because marrying one's purported blackmailer is hardly the action of a grounded man like George Rae with potentially so much to lose.

The Battle Escalates

As the fight for George Rae's wealth rages, newspapers continue their coverage. Elizabeth Rae's life is placed under the microscope.

Further statements to the effect that the late George Rae had told him prior to his marriage to his former housekeeper that he was forced to take that step because he feared she would make trouble for him under the Mann White Slave Act was offered before Judge Tazwell this morning by Edmond G. Amme, Atty & relative by marriage to Rae's 1st wife.

The testimony was introduced in the suit brought by his adopted daughter, [Maud] Rae Emerson, to break the will left by Rae, in which he gave the largest part of his $100,000 estate to his wife, Mrs. Elizabeth E. Rae, leaving Mrs. Emerson but $10.

Rae and his housekeeper traveled over the U.S. and Europe previous to their marriage and it is from these trips that Rae is said to have feared prosecution. Mrs. Rae spent about 3 days on the stand denying that their relations had ever been improper, or that she forced Rae to marry her.

During an era when the mere suggestion of impropriety can tarnish reputations, Elizabeth Rae is subjected to a presumably-hellish three day onslaught that questions her motives and honor. But neither does George Rae's daughter, Maud Rae Emerson, escape unscathed:

Under cross examination this morning, Amme admitted that in her childhood [Maud] Rae, adopted daughter of George Rae and Mrs. Charlotte Rae, who is the contestant of the will, had been "rather wild." Mrs. Rae, in later years of her life developed extreme nervousness and was finally committed to an asylum. Maud Rae, Amme testified, was sent to a convent in Salem and he saw her there many times while he was serving in the legislature.

It was following Maud Rae's marriage to Emerson that George Rae married his former housekeeper. There was some slight friction between Emerson and Rae over the administration of the estate left by the first Mrs. Rae, according to Amme. Emerson was disliked by Rae who made many allowances because of his daughter and in the first testimony of Amme, it was his first intention to leave practically his entire estate to Maud Rae Emerson.

Just when it appears family acrimony can't get worse, on January 21, 1920, a shocking accusation in the Rae case is made public:

WILL CONTEST CITES 'DEADWEIGHT WIFE'

Letters to Late George Rae Introduced in Court

SON-IN-LAW IS AUTHOR

The news story opens with indelicate references to Rae's daughter Maud by T.S. Emerson, George Rae's son-in-law in a letter.

There is one point upon which I would like to refresh your memory. It is that it was not I who asked for your daughter's hand, but it was you who asked me to marry her.

In his defending arguments, Rae estate attorney W.M. Cake states letters like this from T. S. Emerson to his father-in-law George Rae were:

...the direct cause of the old man [George Rae] drawing up a will which cut off his adopted daughter Maud Rae Emerson and her husband with $10 of a $100,000 estate shortly after the receipt of the communications...

Like a one-two punch, T. S. Emerson continues with an especially mean blow in a letter to his father-in-law, George Rae:

There is one thing...to be perfectly frank, and that is that Maud must be able to keep up her end, as my success is in sight and I cannot afford to carry any dead weight, especially as we had all that settled before I married. It would be a different thing had I married a poor man's daughter, but I married a rich man's daughter and under certain conditions.

What T. S. Emerson means by 'dead weight' can only be surmised. His wife Maud may spend more than Emerson likes, or perhaps she has not contributed financially toward the lifestyle he desires. Emerson shifts tactics with another letter to George Rae September 8, 1914:

I am a joint partner in Maud's inheritance...I have told her that it is likely you are sick, but between us I think you are under undue influence...You must remember that there were many things in your life that designate that you have taken precious care of your own selfish interests...

The Oregonian also mentions a pre-nuptial agreement reportedly granting T. S. Emerson half of all property Maud inherits. The newspaper account suggests that Emerson's motives are as transparent as his father-in-law's certain fury:

In the letters which aroused the wrath of Rae, Emerson...attacked acts of Rae in connection with the estate of his late wife [Lottie] in which Emerson felt he had a share through his wife [Maud].

The Oregonian's account further reveals Emerson's strident tone:

Doing anything against Maud cannot hurt me and she will suffer both from you if you neglect her and from me in making you angry at her because she will live only according to her income, so put that in the pipe and smoke it.

Given such ham-fisted tactics, it's difficult to believe T. S. Emerson actually expects his father-in-law to change his mind. Emerson's bravado is evidently seen as a bluff by George Rae. The Oregonian article continues under the sub-heading 'Decision Is Postponed:'

As evidence for proponents and contestants closed yesterday with the exception of the depositions of Mr. and Mrs. [Emerson], which have not been received from Paris, where the couple now are living. Decision on the case was postponed by Circuit [J]udge Tazwell until after arrival and perusal of the depositions.

The letters were written in July and September, 1914, and the will which virtually disinherited Mrs. Emerson was drawn up December 9, 1914. [George & Elizabeth marry November 6, 1914]. *Emerson, it appeared from evidence, had a pre-nuptial agreement by which he was to receive one-half of any property which might be left his wife.*

The chief contention of Mrs. Emerson, contestant, has been that the widow of Rae, who was his housekeeper before marriage and traveled with him all over the United States and Europe, unduly influenced her husband by threats of prosecution under the Mann act or disgrace if she did not receive the bulk of his estate.

Elizabeth Rae and George Rae's long-time attorney, William Cake, both testify that George Rae changes his will because of arguments with T. S. Emerson in the latter half of 1914. An Oregonian article also provides a rare peek into the details of Elizabeth's testimony:

Mrs. Rae, called on the stand in rebuttal yesterday, testified that in her travels with Rae she always paid her own expenses and that she was worth about $15,000 at the time of their trip to Europe together. She positively denied any meretricious relations [prostitution] or passing as his wife before marriage.

During these proceedings, Elizabeth states she receives $25 a month as George Rae's housekeeper. The Oregonian then quotes testimony from an esteemed acquaintance of George Rae. Given this attestant's stellar reputation, what follows gives weight to dismiss the notion that George Rae was manipulated by Elizabeth or anyone else:

R. D. Inman of the Inman-Poulsen Lumber company testified yesterday that Rae, who was in charge of the retail sales of the mill, was a man who was not easily influenced.

Besides the emotional distance between George Rae and his daughter, Maud, Elizabeth Rae's written testimony also suggests a significant geographical distance between the two for quite some time:

That I have known Maud Rae Emerson for a long number of years, to wit, not less than ten or twelve years; that she, the said Maud Rae Emerson has not resided in the City of Portland, or in the State of Oregon, since some time in the year 1913, but in said year married and moved to, and so far as your affiant is aware, has always since said year of 1913, lived in the Republic of France. [Records show that Maud & T. S. Emerson actually marry on August 20, 1912].

Elizabeth Rae's statements to the court continue:

That the said Maud Rae Emerson is the adopted daughter of the first wife of said George Rae, deceased, Lottie Rae; that the said Lottie Rae has relatives, to-wit, a sister, aunt of said Maud Rae Emerson, and daughters of said sister, to-wit, cousins of said Maud Rae Emerson, who live in the City of Portland,

...[Elizabeth Rae] is informed and believes, and therefore alleges that none of said relatives have heard from said Maud Rae Emerson, either directly from herself, or through her husband, since the death of George Rae, and for a considerable time prior...[Elizabeth Rae] is informed and believes and therefore alleges, that...[Emerson attorney] Arthur C. Spencer has not heard from...Maud Rae Emerson and has not authority of any kind to appear or represent her or to institute the proceeding in contest of the Last Will and Testament of George Rae, deceased;

That the last time George Rae in his life time heard from said Maud Rae Emerson was in the latter part of the year 1914, and at no time thereafter and until his death, did he receive any communication from or hear directly or indirectly from said Maud Rae Emerson.

Counter-Attack

The Rae camp has a few tactics of their own to keep the Emerson legal team off balance. Since plaintiffs T. S. & Maud Rae Emerson reside in France, Rae estate attorney J.

A. Strowbridge argues that the Emerson's lead attorney at the time, A. C. Spencer, has had no contact or authority from his clients. Strowbridge reasons Spencer therefore can't represent the two who challenge Elizabeth's claim to her husband's estate, let alone file claims on their behalf.

Emerson attorney A. C. Spencer is asked to provide proof of his authority to represent Maud Emerson by April 12, 1919, or dismiss the case. Given the challenge and unreliability of trans-oceanic communications, this puts the Emerson legal team in an unenviable position. Other options to prove legitimate authority in representing Maud and T. S. Emerson include sharing their embarrassingly candid letters with the court, or remain silent and risk having the case thrown out.

Attorney A. C. Spencer's creative response is an affidavit to help establish his legitimacy as legal counsel for Maud Rae Emerson. In it, he cites his prior position as her attorney during George Rae's lifetime. This includes Spencer's earlier work for the Emersons on litigation against Maud's father, George Rae, in challenging the estate of his deceased wife, Charlotte.

Attorney Spencer's affidavit concedes that the bulk of his communications are with Maud's husband, T. S. Emerson. Then Spencer reveals more, including written authorization from Maud Rae Emerson to help establish Spencer's legitimacy to represent her in a letter dated February 2, 1915:

Mr. Arthur C. Spencer,
510 Wells Fargo Building,
Portland, Oregon, U.S.A.

Dear Sir:-

*I beg to advise you that at all times either the
direction suggested, in the matter of the Rae Estate and all
that pertains thereunto, by my husband T. S. Emerson or my
father-in-law H.S. Emerson is to be followed absolutely and
entirely and is to my approved satisfaction.*

> *Very respectfully,*
> *(Signed) Maud Emerson.*

But that's not all Emerson attorney A. C. Spencer
releases to the court. To leave little doubt of their legal
relationship, Spencer quotes liberally from a letter he
receives from T. S. Emerson dated May 23, 1918. This letter
helps to confirm Spencer's legitimacy in continuing to
represent his clients, but also says much more:

*As in the past everything is left in your [Spencer's]
hands to act as you think best, and if any of our ideas help so
much the better, and if not there is nothing lost.*

T. S. Emerson's soliloquy continues in his letter
with a brazen attempt to impugn Elizabeth's character:

*In the will did George Rae cut off Mrs. Maud
Emerson, who is the person who has the best rights, in favor
of Mrs. Rae 2nd? If so, why? Did she ever do anything
against him? No. Or was it again undue influence over an
old sick man?*

*Since Mrs. Maxwell or Mrs. Rae 2nd appeared on
the scene she has exercised a certain influence over Mr. Rae
in as much as she kept him away from his daughter and
instead of letting her take up her home with him permanently
had her sent to a convent...when she was too old for that he
allowed a small sum per month and only saw her rarely and
at her insistent request and at these times Mrs. Rae 2nd who*

111

was then only a housekeeper and bore the name of Mrs. Maxwell and who had no ligitimate [sic] right to act in this manner. She was only his wife after 6 months from the demise of Mrs. Charlotte Rae which took place some time in 1913—(I believe).

T. S. Emerson's statement is not entirely accurate, for Charlotte "Lottie" Rae dies January 12, 1914 and George Rae remarries November 6, 1914, approximately ten months, not six, after Lottie's death. T.S. Emerson then concludes with his own theory of events:

Of course, if by any chance the will of George Rae is reasonable we would be wasting time and money to fight it. But I have my doubts of that will. Mr. Rae was especially bitter to me because I was frank enough to tell him that he did not live up to his word and he knew it and that is what made him mad and without doubt caused Mrs. Maxwell to exert her influence over him [and] have him cancel his daughter's allowance which he solemnly promised to never cancel. Mrs. Rae 2nd appears to want it all. Why don[']t they want Mrs. Maud E. to have hers?

Although the Rae legal team places the plaintiffs squarely on the defensive, the court approves A.C. Spencer's legitimacy in representing Maud and T. S. Emerson.

The Wait

To summarize the Emerson legal team's position, they claim unfair treatment from George Rae, beginning with the outcome of Charlotte Rae's estate. George Rae's son-in-law and daughter are still stinging from his rebuke six years earlier, given their meager portion from Lottie Rae's estate. Now in challenging George Rae's will, they seek to avoid a replay. At this point, the court waits for depositions from the

Emersons living in Paris.

Maud and T. S. Emerson have reason to be concerned, for their track record in pursuing the Rae riches is indeed mixed. With a notarized, yet legally indeterminate will favoring Elizabeth Rae, their odds remain dicey. Rae attorney W. M. Cake thrusts and parries in an effort to buy time, catch the plaintiffs off guard and end litigation. What comes out next are T. S. Emerson's seemingly specific expectations in marrying Maud Rae. With the subheading "Letter Quotations Cited," an article in The Oregonian details one of Emerson's letters to George Rae:

I can tell you that since we have been in France she [Maud] has cost me a great deal more than what you have sent her. Of course she tries hard and does the best that she can but there is one point upon which I would like to refresh your memory.

Emerson continues, simultaneously invoking sympathy with each hurled accusation:

I told you at the time I did not wish to take a wife to support as I was a poor young man and had an ambition to go to Paris but would rather wait a couple of years, but you said never mind that, I will give Maud at least $100 a month and a little later when you are ready to go in business I will help you.

Still fishing for pity, Emerson attempts to set the hook with a timber analogy for his lumber baron father-in-law:

The first you have done, but the second—well, you have said that you were hard up, etc; I have said nothing but sawed wood. It has been a very hard struggle with me and the going has been slow compared with what it might have been had I had the support you promised. If you think that I have so much the best of it.

Emerson follows with a cutting remark that unleashes a new phase in the fighting. This begins a "no-holds barred" strategy accompanied by T. S. Emerson's thinly-veiled threat to leave his own wife, Rae's daughter:

I can make arrangements for Maud to live by herself, or if you wish it you can have her return to live with you.

This single sentence ensures T. S. Emerson has his father-in-law's attention. Yet in fighting fire with fire, Emerson relentlessly stokes the white hot coals of enmity, not expecting to get burned half way around the globe in France. In his letters to Rae, Emerson's choice of words could hardly be more incendiary. It's as difficult to believe his intent is to persuade, as it is to read without cringing.

George Rae may have reneged on an earlier promise to his son-in-law. But Emerson composes letters so caustic as to virtually guarantee a negative response. Treating financial support from an in-law as a debt to be paid is unusual. Yet Emerson is so focused on Rae's money, he appears oblivious to any sense of decorum. On September 8, 1914, The Oregonian corroborates T. S. Emerson's promise between himself and George Rae:

Emerson, it appeared from evidence, had a pre-nuptial agreement by which he was to receive one-half of any property which might be left his wife.

T. S. Emerson's behavior might initially be dismissed as a youthful indiscretion. But his actions are as patterned and premeditated as Emerson's own prenuptial arrangement. Whether naïve or simply angry, Emerson's effort to liberate funds with bombastic barrages has the opposite effect.

Final Letter Dated in 1914

According to the Oregonian newspaper, T.S. Emerson's last letter to his father-in-law George Rae is dated September 15, 1914. The missive's tone is matter-of-fact, the intent clear:

To be perfectly plain I can support a wife, but the point with me is that I feel I have been imposed upon in this case by different promises you made me before we were married. I took a great responsibility off your hands when I married her...Then I found after I married, the reputation of your family would not help me any and I was glad to get away from Portland. You know what I mean.

What is Emerson saying about George Rae? On more than one occasion, Emerson stops short of revealing what he alludes to know about his father-in-law. Emerson's cryptic blackmail reveals a man willing to leverage a sensitive situation for money. Still, threats do not sway Rae. The Oregonian reveals more:

The chief contention of Mrs. Emerson, contestant, has been that the widow of Rae, who was his housekeeper before marriage and traveled with him all over the United States and Europe, unduly influenced her husband by threats of prosecution under the Mann act or disgrace if she did not receive the bulk of his estate.

Blind with frustration, Emerson doesn't seem to grasp the effect his letters have on his father-in-law. In anger, he mistakenly believes George Rae can be intimidated. Like many sons-in-law before and since, Emerson's fate is sealed by allegations of George Rae's shortcomings. As Emerson's browbeating continues, Rae responds like one convinced of his own righteousness and stands firm.

Chapter XI: The End Game

On February 13, 1919 in a court document called
"Petition And Complaint In Contest," George Rae's daughter
Maud levels charges against Elizabeth, Rae's widow. The
accusations are serious:

*...George Rae was acting under the coercion,
duress, undue influence, misrepresentations and fraud of said
Elizabeth E. Rae...Elizabeth E. Rae procured said George
Rae to execute said will in her favor and to disinherit your
petitioner by force, coercion, duress, misrepresentations, and
fraud practiced upon...George Rae, and by false and
fraudulent statements and beliefs created in the mind of said
George Rae against your petitioner, Maud Emerson Rae...*

The accusations are unflinching and personal:

*...that for a number of years prior to the execution
of said will and prior to the pretended marriage of said
George Rae and the said Elizabeth E. Rae, the relations
between said George Rae and Elizabeth E. Rae had been
meretricious...*

Surpassing a mere family squabble, Elizabeth's very
honor is stridently called into question:

*...Elizabeth E. Rae had through said relations
secured from the said George Rae large sums of money and
had forced...George Rae to convey her property of large
value and had by coercion and threats placed...George Rae
in fear of her and had induced him by such means to
disregard his obligation and duty towards your petitioner
and had poisoned the mind of said George Rae against your
petitioner and had induced him and attempted to compel him
to transfer a large amount of his property to her [Elizabeth]
and to execute the will in question so that ...Elizabeth E. Rae*

should inherit and acquire the property of...George Rae to the exclusion of our petitioner [Maud Rae Emerson].

The Emerson legal team follows this attack with a hard-to-substantiate claim, suggesting a counterfeit will has replaced the original:

That prior to the execution of said will, said deceased had made a will in which practically the entire estate of said deceased had been left to your petitioner, and that if it had not been for the undue influence and coercion of the said Elizabeth E. Rae, your petitioner would have inherited practically all of the estate of said deceased...

Unsure of their own legal marksmanship, the Emerson team strains credulity as they search for a target:

That the exact provisions and contents of such prior will is not able to state, but alleges that the said Elizabeth E. Rae had access to the safety deposit box of the said deceased, George Rae, and abstracted therefrom numerous papers either immediately prior or subsequent to the death of said George Rae, but your petitioner is informed and believes that the contents thereof can be established in case the same has been destroyed...

Given such a buildup, the summary seems mild:

...that the said pretended will dated December 9, 1914, is void and should be cancelled and annulled by this Honorable Court for the reasons above set forth.

In a court document dated February 13, 1919, the Emerson team demands that the Rae estate's beneficiaries show why George Rae's contested will should not be disallowed and ask Rae's Widow to:

...produce said prior will, and in case the original of said will cannot be produced, that the same be reestablished and probated as and for the last will and testament of said George Rae, or in case the same cannot be reestablished, that said estate be administered and our petitioner be given the share thereof as provided by the laws of the State of Oregon, and your petitioner will ever pray.

Signing for petitioner Maud Rae Emerson is her attorney, A. C. Spencer. That same day, Judge Tazwell issues an 'alias citation' that calls for parties with an interest in the Rae estate to appear before the court on the morning of March 1, 1919. Named are Rae Estate executor George Thatcher, George Rae's wife Elizabeth and Rae's relatives James and William Rae. Those served are required to show cause why George Rae's will dated December 9, 1914 should not be set aside.

The citations are mailed and their contents published in the local Sunday Welcome newspaper, where it first appears on April 5, 1919. James Rae lives in Harbor, Oregon, near Brookings on the southern Oregon coast. William Rae is a resident of faraway Toronto, Canada. Judge Tazwell's order requires James Rae to appear by May 1, 1919. The court recognizes the great distance required for William Rae, brother of the deceased to travel and gives him until June 2, 1919 to complete his journey.

The hearing is held and the court rules that George Rae's will not be set aside. In other words, the will before the court will be determined on its own merits. By this time, George Rae has been deceased for well over one year. The long-awaited decision in the Emerson-Rae war is announced on September 8, 1920 in the form of a decree:

...based upon said findings of fact and conclusions of law, it is ordered, adjudged and decreed that the document

*offered and accepted in evidence as the last will and
testament of George Rae, deceased, is, and the same is
hereby declared to be, the last will and testament of the said
George Rae, deceased, and that said last will and testament
be, and the same is hereby, admitted to probate in solemn
form...*

Judge Tazwell's findings are so unambiguous he
practically places a bow on this once untidy package and
grants Elizabeth clear absolution:

*...the allegations set forth in...the contestants'
petition and complaint in contest are untrue, and that in
executing the said will...to the said George Rae was not
subjected to any coercion, duress, undue influence,
misrepresentation or fraud by Elizabeth Rae, his wife, or any
other person...*

But still, the Emersons keep litigation alive. In new
accusations they charge Elizabeth with, among other things,
transferring property to unnamed parties to avoid scrutiny of
the court:

*...George Rae left a residuary estate not devised or
bequeathed by said pretended Will, and your petitioner will
inherit from said estate.*

Supreme Court: The Final Round

The Emerson legal team appeals Judge Tazwell's
decision, all the way to the Oregon Supreme Court. As a
result, a settlement is soon reached. Maud and T. S. Emerson
receive one property from George Rae's estate and the back
rents that go with it. In exchange, they agree to withdraw all
further legal challenges. After this legal battle royal, the case

of Emerson v. Rae is ordered closed of record by Judge
Tazwell:

*In the Circuit Court of the State of Oregon for
Multnomah County*

Contest Order-

In the Matter of the Estate of George Rae, Deceased

*The above contest having been appealed to the
Supreme Court and having been settled-*

*It is ordered that all exhibits offered in the above
contest may be withdrawn from the files of this court and
delivered to James G. Wilson of attorneys for contestant for
delivery to the parties entitled thereto.*

*Done and dated in open court this 14th day of
October 1920-*

(signed)
George Tazwell
Judge

On The Trail of T. S. Emerson

Having researched the Emerson-Rae duel for years
by now, I'm left scratching my head. Through it all,
questions remain, but they're different ones than when I
began. Having learned a great deal about George Rae, I
realize his actions were often predictable. More challenging
is figuring out T. S. Emerson, who seems to have been such a
driven and angry guy. Surely George Rae's son-in-law had
some redeeming qualities as well.

To be fair toward T. S. Emerson, I decide to review his will and estate information in hopes they might provide a more balanced perspective. I also reason Emerson may well have changed later in life. For only $25, it's a safe bet. Attached with my payment to the appropriate government agency is a note with what I know. It includes Emerson's full name, date of death, and last known residence. I drop everything in the mail, then wait and ponder. Where is T. S. Emerson buried? Is it lavish like the Rae tomb? And what happens to Emerson's money, which he so desperately fights to amass?

A month or so later, I receive a wad of papers. The manila packet bearing my name is so thick, I'm required to pay extra postage. It's well worth the price of admission as it opens windows wide into the mind of one who went toe-to-toe with George Rae.

LAST WILL AND TESTAMENT

of

THEODORE S. EMERSON

I, THEODORE S. EMERSON, of Seattle, King County, State of Washington, being of the age of majority and of sound and disposing mind and memory and not acting under any restraint, duress, fraud or influence of any person, circumstance of matter whatsoever, do freely and voluntarily make, publish and declare this my Last Will and Testament, and I do hereby revoke all other wills by me heretofore made.

FIRST: I hereby direct that my Executrix pay all of my debts and funeral.

SECOND: I desire that my remains be cremated at the Bonney Watson Funeral Parlors, provided their price is competitive. It is my express wish that the funeral services in all respects be handled in a modest manner and that the expense involved be kept to a reasonable minimum. I further request that the services at the funeral be of the simplest nature and request that my attorney, John E. Linde, officiate at the services and say that 'the deceased did the best he could under the circumstances.' It is further my wish that my ashes be scattered with the ashes of my mother and father in the front yard of my home at 2823 - 31st Avenue South, Seattle, Washington, except that some of the ashes be saved and scattered on the Grands boulevards of Paris and also scattered on the Promenade des Anglais at Nice.

Paging through the document, I stop at a later section. There for the first time, T. S. Emerson seems compassionate. Even more surprising, he's also a bit humble:

SEVENTH: I hereby give, devise and bequeath all the rest, residue and remainder of my estate whether real, personal and/or mixed and wherever situated of which I may die seized or possessed to my beloved wife, Germaine A. Emerson, who has supported all of my idiosyncrasies and who has exercised great sympathy for all when my temper has not been all it should have been. [She is] a most marvelous creature who has had the patience of an angel and who has always willingly endured and supported all my faults.

As I sift through these old pages sporting Emerson's name, they conjure a vaguely visceral notion of the man. My limited impression of T. S. Emerson remains a gloomy one. How else to describe behavior of one so money-conscious as to admit marrying for it? Emerson's will ends with assorted directives for the disposal of his estate. Dated November 27th, 1942, that is, oddly enough, little more than three weeks before Elizabeth Rae's own death. It's but another strange irony in this whole story. Decades after their epic battle, the two who fought so hard for the Rae estate both die at virtually the same time.

T. S. Emerson's estate is appraised at $49,076.15. All but about $5,000 goes to his wife, Germaine Emerson. After reading the Final Report and Petition for Distribution of Emerson's estate, I have to go over it again to make sure I'm not mistaken. Mouth agape while silently shaking my head, I'm not.

THIRD: I hereby give and bequeath to my daughter, Evelyn M. Emerson, $100.00. In the event that my daughter, Evelyn M. Emerson, is not living at the time of my death, this bequest is void and the sum mentioned shall become a part of the body of my estate.

In life, T. S. Emerson fiercely attacks George Rae for not gifting Rae's daughter—Emerson's wife—more money from Rae's will. In death, Emerson behaves like the father-in-law he battled a quarter century earlier. That's because Rae wills just $10 to his daughter Maud, and Emerson leaves his daughter Evelyn but $100. Each man leaves his wife the the lion's share. But unlike court testimony explaining George Rae's rationale, I can find no reason for Emerson to essentially write his daughter out of his will.

Epilogue

Buckling my seatbelt on the flight to Scotland, I feel a reassuring calm. After years of researching the life and death of George Rae, in April, 2003 I have the opportunity to tour his native land. While unsure what to expect on the trip, I know it should be interesting and am not disappointed. In the process, I develop a taste for haggis and neeps (a traditional Scottish dish of spiced meat and turnips), witness the beautiful Scottish countryside and walk the streets of Ellon, George Rae's home town. The resemblance of northern Scotland to parts of Oregon is obvious. The Willamette Valley must have reminded George Rae of his former home.

Ellon is a picturesque and pedestrian-friendly village. Bordered on one side by the peaceful Ythian River, the town is small enough to walk around in half an hour. While a lot has changed since Rae was a boy, I'm told the luscious green valley, rolling hills and river in the heart of downtown are much the same. Restaurants, hotels and friendly shops still cluster around the old city centre, with a church, library, local newspaper, plus pubs, parks and a nearby athletic club.

My wife Laurie and I find Ellon a pleasant and tidy little town and the people gracious. Walking about, I begin searching for links—however tenuous—to the beginning of the Rae story. Having studied fruit from his family tree, it's a unique opportunity to observe what might remain of the roots.

Ready with a few pages in my pocket about George Rae's Scottish relatives, we spot a cemetery on the outskirts of town and walk through it. Amazingly enough, we find the gravestones of George Rae's sisters. Since we're scheduled to be in Scotland for only a few days, I had earnestly hoped to find more before we have to leave. But no one buried in that cemetery is old enough to be George Rae's parents.

As we reach the far end of the cemetery, I remember passing the town church on our way through. We drive the short distance back and park the car. There, I see lots of gravestones behind a sturdy and aged stone fence. These are much older. Strolling through the cemetery, I eventually locate the weathered grave marker of John and Isabelle Rae. The tall tablet is old and hard to read. Yet, like the legacy of their son who journeys far so long ago, it still stands.

Loose Ends

After years of legal wrangling, the estate of lumber baron George Rae is settled. But what of the intriguing participants who vie for the Rae riches? Over time I've found some details about T. S. Emerson, but are there any loose ends? Indeed, there are.

A little more digging reveals that prior to his death, Emerson leaves wife Maud behind in France, then remarries and establishes himself in Seattle to learn his father's successful commission brokerage business. A self-described 'purchasing and sales agent' for Alaska merchants, Emerson eventually establishes his own firm, the Alaska Brokerage Company in February 1939. Emerson's timing is poor, as this is mere months before Hitler invades Poland, touching off the outbreak of World War II in Europe.

Yet, for T. S. Emerson and his young company, the war abroad seems distant, at least for a while. He follows in his enterprising father's footsteps, shipping food and supplies north from Seattle to Alaska in these years before statehood. After Pearl Harbor is attacked on December 7, 1941, west coast shipping is particularly vulnerable and Emerson's once-promising company begins to suffer.

The U.S. government makes matters worse for private companies like the Alaska Brokerage Company by appropriating materials for the war effort. This means Emerson must compete with the government, both in procuring goods and shipping them. On July 22, 1941, Emerson outlines his concerns in a letter to his client W. Stoll, manager of Alaska Pacific Cons. Mining Co.:

...You no doubt read the latest news in regard to the Government [requisitioning] anything that they desire to. We learned from one of our friends in the quarter master's department at Seattle that they are liable to go through the jobber's stocks and help themselves. It seems that the canners cannot supply them with sufficient quantities of all the stuff they want. We are advising you...to have you get your fall order in as promptly as possible so that we can mark the cases in the warehouse and have them listed as sold in case the Government steps in. Please do not delay this as it is very important...

Such government intervention deals a death blow to Emerson's business just prior to his actual death. T. S. Emerson dies on April 25, 1943, less than one month after his Alaska Brokerage Company, Inc. is officially dissolved. Three and a half years later, his wife Germaine brings it back into existence by re-incorporating under the virtually identical name of Alaska Brokerage Company. That firm is finally dissolved in 1957.

Because T. S. Emerson's ashes are scattered and his known relatives are deceased, little more can be found about him. Discussions with distant family associates provide a few glimpses resembling the man whose trail I've followed. I'm also told that Maud Rae Emerson is likely buried in France.

While French records can be incredibly difficult to access, I locate one photo of an elderly woman purported to be Maud in France. She allegedly loves again, her final days spent battling diabetes and poor eyesight within walking distance of Notre Dame.

What Happens To Inman-Poulsen?

The 1929-1930 Capitol's 'Who's Who for Oregon' acknowledges the Inman-Poulsen Lumber Company under then-President Henry Brooks Van Duzer as:

...one of the best known in the state of Oregon and one of the oldest in continuous operation...

Decades after its founding, the company's plant is described as then covering:

...about 60 acres...[with]...several logging camps in the state. The mill's location is noted as S. E. Carruthers [sic] St. in Portland.

Industries change with time. Some, like buggy whip makers, vanish. Others, such as shipbuilders, find cheaper labor elsewhere and sometimes set up shop overseas. Still others, like lumber firms, are often absorbed by larger companies. That's what happens to Inman-Poulsen.

The Inman-Poulsen Lumber Company's story is seemingly far removed in time and place from the Civil War. Yet, Inman-Poulsen co-founder R. D. Inman's father fights for The Union cause and loses his life during the Battle of Shiloh. Interestingly, the man to eventually engineer the Inman-Poulsen Lumber Company's takeover also sports Civil War lineage, but with opposing Confederate ties.

This is because the maternal line of a key Georgia Pacific executive is linked to the Boisseau family, reported owners of a 600 acre plantation named Tudor Hall. The estate is said to have once been worked by up to 50 slaves.

R. Boisseau Pamplin, Sr. is involved with the buyout of Inman-Poulsen by Georgia-Pacific Lumber Company in 1954. Ironic indeed, that an Oregon company co-founded over half a century earlier by R. D. Inman, a Union soldier's son, is dissolved largely through efforts of R. B. Pamplin, Sr., an executive with Confederate heritage.

Final Thoughts

This adventure began simply when I walked into a magnificent tomb and was intrigued. In examining such a story, it's important to remember these lives were not immune to problems and suffering, yet remain instructive with poignant lessons.

Given the luxury of historical hindsight, distinct patterns appear throughout George Rae's remarkable life. His response to adversity and opportunity reveals character, strengths and sure enough, flaws. Passing through life ahead of us in imperfect humanity, records of his journey illustrate what we, too are capable of achieving.

Though he travels through some of life's darkest valleys, George Rae also climbs atop the highest of life's mountains and makes it all look easy. He blazes his own fascinating trail for all who care to explore it, hence this book.

An examination of Rae's life teaches important lessons, as he accomplishes many things. Rather than squander his talents, he stays the course and adjusts as necessary, while keeping his eyes ever on the goal at hand. George Rae's rise from inauspicious beginnings, his ability to discern opportunity, and undeniable resolve in the face of adversity belie his humanity.

Made in the USA
Monee, IL
07 November 2020

46907696R00075